GLASGOW'S GREAT EXHIBITIONS
1888·1901·1911·1938·1988

Perilla Kinchin (b. 1951) studied Classics at Newnham College, Cambridge, Victoria, BC, and Oxford, and until recently has been a Lecturer in Classics at Trinity and Merton Colleges, Oxford. She is married to E. L. Bowie, an Oxford don, and has two young sons.

Juliet Kinchin (b. 1956) also read Classics at Cambridge before switching to History of Art. After taking an MA at the Courtauld Institute, London, and working at the Victoria and Albert Museum, she joined Glasgow Museums and Art Galleries in 1980 as Assistant Keeper with responsibility for Pollok House. She is now director of the newly established Christie's Scotland Programme in the Decorative Arts at the University of Glasgow.

Neil Baxter (b. 1960) took his MA in the History of Art and English Literature at the University of Glasgow. He is currently the Assistant Secretary of the Royal Incorporation of Architects in Scotland, and a part-time lecturer at the Mackintosh School of Architecture, Glasgow. He is a regular contributor to *Books in Scotland*.

GLASGOW'S GREAT EXHIBITIONS
1888·1901·1911·1938·1988

PERILLA KINCHIN AND JULIET KINCHIN

With a contribution by Neil Baxter

White
Cockade

White Cockade Publishing
Wendlebury House, Church Lane
Wendlebury, Bicester
Oxon OX6 8PN

British Library Cataloguing in Publication Data

Kinchin, Perilla, *1951-*
    Glasgow's Great Exhibitions: 1888, 1901, 1911, 1938, 1988.
    1. Scotland. Strathclyde Region. Exhibitions, 1888-1988
    I. Title   II. Kinchin, Juliet   III. Baxter, Neil, *1960-*
060

    ISBN 0-9513124-0-5

Designed by Gerald Cinamon, Cinamon and Kitzinger
Typeset in 11 on 13½ point Lasercomp Ehrhardt
at the Oxford University Computing Service
Printed and bound in Scotland by Bell and Bain, Glasgow

Front cover: R. G. Coventry (1855-1914), *1901 Exhibition,*
Kelvingrove, Glasgow (courtesy of Barclay Lennie)
Back cover: Hugh Watt, *The Tower of Empire* (used in 1937
for an official Christmas card: courtesy of William Topping)
Frontispiece: John Lavery (1856-1941), *Glasgow Exhibition, 1888*
(courtesy of Glasgow Art Gallery and Museum, Kelvingrove)

For Ewen,
who has put up with a lot

CONTENTS

PREFACE

In 1988, exactly one hundred years after the first International Exhibition to be held in Glasgow in 1888, and fifty years after the great Empire Exhibition of 1938, the city is staging Britain's third National Garden Festival. Within this span also fall the second International Exhibition of 1901 and the Scottish National Exhibition of 1911.

It has been a century of profound social and economic change in the city, from industrial prosperity through steep decline to promised resurgence. The fortunes of Glasgow have reflected those of Britain at large in a particularly intense way. The five great shows we look at in these pages offer insights of a specially appealing kind into society and its changing ethos and needs. They have been mounted each time in a characteristic fling of confidence and have left behind many happy memories.

Universal exhibitions have attempted with matchless optimism to enclose the diversity of human knowledge and endeavour in one place. This we cannot emulate in writing about them, even if we had wished to be exhaustive. Instead we have attempted an survey which will stimulate interest in a rather splendid phenomenon, and a tradition of which Glasgow can be particularly proud. We must apologise to anyone with a special passion for, say, ship models, or Australian wine, if the amount of detail we give is unfairly tantalising.

While we have said nothing without evidence we know that this does not guarantee truth. There is a basic difficulty here: one is often dealing with facts from accounts prepared in advance of the actual Exhibitions, or garbled by reporters. Exhibitions were assembled under pressure and they changed in progress. A few discrepancies have been unresolvable. Our own chapter on the Garden Festival 1988 has been written before the event and is subject to these problems: for this reason our coverage does not attempt to give a complete description but concentrates rather on features of the enterprise which set it in the tradition of the Exhibitions and differentiate it from them.

The chapter on 1938 is almost entirely the work of Neil Baxter, based on the researches for his thesis *Thomas S. Tait and the Glasgow Empire Exhibition 1938*. We are extremely grateful to him for all the material he has provided, and also to Andrew Baxter for his painstaking redrawing of the maps.

To Barclay Lennie and Dr Ian Evans we owe a debt which cannot be standing. Stanley Hunter has also given us invaluable information. We have many others to thank for help of many kinds: Roger Billcliffe, Ewen Bowie, Chris Carrell, Jerry Cinamon, Jasper Gaunt, George and Barbara Kinchin, Dr Peter Mackenzie, Mark O'Neill and Susan Scott; and on behalf of Neil Baxter Sandy Allan, Andrew Baxter, Charles McKean and William Topping. Of many who have helped in connection with the Garden Festival special thanks go to Ray Alexander, Richard Cunningham, and Jim McFarlane; to Graeme Currie and Bovis Construction Ltd; Sue Jones and Gillespie's; Ian Bruce and Bruce, Patience and Wernham; and David Leslie and Walter Underwood and Partners. We thank too the staff of the Archives, the Special Collections, and the Hunterian Art Gallery of the University of Glasgow; the Glasgow Art Gallery and Museum, Kelvingrove; the People's Palace; the Cecil Higgins Art Gallery, Bedford; and above all Mr J. A. Fisher and the librarians of the wonderful Glasgow Room of the Mitchell Library.

Needless to say we find these Exhibitions completely fascinating, and would be delighted to hear from anyone with interesting material stored in private papers or living memory: these personal details bring the past alive better than anything else.

P. K. M. K.
J. L. C. K.

INTRODUCTION

Exhibitions on the grand scale began in London with the Crystal Palace of 1851. Their origins can of course be traced back further, to the long-established human institution of the fair, when people gathered from far and wide in holiday spirits to buy and sell and gape at side-shows; or to the large industrial fairs held in France from the very end of the eighteenth century; or more immediately to the series of exhibitions giving prominence to good design staged in 1847, 1848 and 1849 by the Royal Society of Arts in London. But the 'Great Exhibition of the Works of Industry of all Nations' in its vast building of iron and glass was something of a new and different order.

The 1851 Exhibition had an overwhelming effect. Over six million passed soberly through the admission gates, and prophesies of riot, plague and the certain collapse of Joseph Paxton's unprecedented structure were forgotten in a surge of patriotic pride. The massed displays of 'all that is useful and beautiful in nature or in art', of the world's riches and man's ingenuity combined, evoked a powerful sense of wonder and gratitude, often expressed in religious terms. Although commercial and national interests were well served by the Exhibition, its international scope and idealistic commitment to the advancement of art and industry were the essential ingredients. There were no amusements, no smoking, no alcohol (and no dogs), and refreshments were limited and expensive. But the Exhibition was an unqualified success and made substantial profits, which, shrewdly managed, have been used ever since by the Royal Commission to promote education in design and science. So began a veritable craze for large exhibitions, expositions or world's fairs, as they were variously called.

Exhibitions can be seen as the natural expression of many of the special characteristics of the Victorian era. For one thing they would have been impossible without the railways: the Great Exhibition indeed inaugurated a new age of excursion tourism. Unlike fairs they were entirely respectable and appealed in a way matched only by Royalty (who were generally required to open them) to all ages and classes of a highly stratified population. But above all they embodied those values we think of as Victorian, that is, the tastes, attitudes and practical dynamism of the new middle classes of a new consumer society.

Foremost of these values was an unclouded confidence in progress and the onward march of civilisation, in the white man's capacity to exploit and control the wealth given him by God. The universal exhibition comfortingly confirmed the belief that all resources, all knowledge, all culture could be categorised, labelled and enclosed in an orderly manner. Here was the whole world tidied up and brought to the doorstep. The attitudes embodied were strongly imperial and chauvinistic: countries divided clearly into those which exhibited and those which were exhibited. Subject peoples appeared reassuringly tame, while rival world powers observed the etiquette of harmonious and peaceful relations within the exhibition.

Competitiveness and materialism were at the heart of the system. Like museums, sharing the celebration of the artefact, large exhibitions have flourished in western, or westernised, capitalist manufacturing centres. Medals were awarded at the earlier exhibitions for the purpose of selecting by direct comparison the best article in a given class, but the practice was generally abandoned when it began to cause more bad feeling than it was worth. The commercial benefit of exhibiting on these occasions was always apparent, and indeed essential to the whole enterprise. Major exhibitions afforded an international shop-window for display to general public and industry alike and were in effect gigantic bazaars or trade fairs, though such an imputation was always indignantly rejected by their organisers.

For exhibitions were also genuinely educational. They fed very successfully the Victorian appetite for self-improvement - which was often a straightforward curiosity not easily satisfied by other means. It is easy to overlook their importance in the dissemination of ideas and information before the advent of the mass media.

Of course what visitors were ultimately seeking was novelty and entertainment: education then as now cloaked this motive for those of a Puritan disposition. Exhibitions offered another world - colourful, illuminated, full of things strange and wonderful. They offered escape, if temporary, from the dreary sameness or dispiriting shabbiness of generally very constricted lives. Architecture had *carte blanche* for inventiveness: buildings had only to keep out the rain for six summer months, and with no test of time to withstand they could be dedicated to providing a pleasurably spectacular environment. Straightforward amusement sections soon appeared and became increasingly important for the financial viability of exhibitions.

Keen imitators of the Great Exhibition found, however, that it was by no means easy to emulate its success, with leaking roofs, late openings and financial difficulties to contend with. But escalation was uncheckable as city vied with city, nation with nation to stage an exhibition which was at least in some respect 'bigger and better', more astounding, than anything seen before. The London Exhibition of 1862 topped the attendance in 1851 with 6.2 million visitors; after that Paris managed 6.8 million in 1867 and went on to become the world's premier exhibition city for the rest of the nineteenth century with major events in 1878 (16 million), 1889 (32.4 million) and 1900 (48 million).

12

Glasgow entered the lists relatively late, when exhibition activity was reaching its peak in the 1880s, and embarked with the energy of industrial maturity on what was to prove a highly successful career in the field. Many characteristics of the city have found an outlet in its Great Exhibitions: its manufacturing and trading economy, its entrepreneurial outlook, fierce pride, vigorous municipal government and commitment to 'culture for the people'. The first International Exhibition in 1888 had an attendance of almost 5.75 million; this was doubled to about 11.5 million in the International Exhibition of 1901, which was the largest Britain had seen; the Scottish Exhibition of 1911 drew almost 9.5 million; and in a decade of depression attendance topped 12.5 million, two and a half times the population of Scotland, at the Empire Exhibition in 1938. It remains to be seen what total the Garden Festival of 1988 will record: the post-war revolution in communications and leisure patterns is reflected in the expectation that it will be visited by 'only' 4 million. If only because of their scale these events deserve an attention they have not yet been accorded.

It is a tribute to native acumen that Glasgow's first three Exhibitions made good profits. This was no mean feat when huge losses at many international fairs (e.g. Vienna 1873, Paris 1878, St Louis 1904) were effectively written off against national or, in the case of the USA, state prestige, which had soon become heavily involved. Glasgow in 1938 was a different case - though here the appalling summer weather was chiefly to blame; and even then the loss was nothing approaching that at Wembley in 1924-5. In the disturbed era which followed the shattering experience of World War I, exhibitions had become scarcer and their motivation more complex. Government initiative was important in 1938 (though the event was still largely funded by local guarantors) and 'profits' could be seen in terms of the general economic and psychological boost afforded by such a lavish splash. The same is true to a much greater extent today, and the Garden Festival is certain to bring substantial benefits of this sort to Glasgow and its region, while there is no expectation that the basic costs, borne entirely by the taxpayer, will be met by revenues.

Though the balance of the different elements has shifted on each occasion, Glasgow's five big events have shared the mutually reinforcing aims of all major exhibitions: to promote industry and commerce; to attract tourism; to educate; to entertain; and in general to project the city's identity and enhance its prestige.

It is perhaps this last motive which has been the special driving force behind Glasgow's Exhibitions. Since the days of its too rapid growth from what was described in 1764 as 'one of the most beautiful small towns in Europe', into the sprawling, smoking 'Workshop of the World', the city has had problems with its image. From its claim a century ago to be 'Second City of Empire' to the recent 'Glasgow's Miles Better' campaign, aggressive self-promotion has always been necessary, in the face of an outside world horrified by tales of the squalor of its slums, and snobbishly disdainful of the industrial associations of its cultural wealth. It was and is felt that if ignorant outsiders would only come and look, they would certainly be impressed. Exhibitions are essentially acts of corporate boasting, and in Glasgow's case tap a particularly rich vein of civic pride: they have an obvious rôle to play in the struggle for national and international status.

Perhaps at last Glasgow's message has got across. The breakthrough has been made on several fronts, particularly by the opening of the Burrell Collection in 1983, and the eminence of the city's art galleries, museums, music, opera, theatre and less formal arts has been widely acknowledged. Glasgow can take justifiable satisfaction in its nomination as European City of Culture in 1990, an accolade particularly pleasurable for the irritation it caused in Edinburgh. The Garden Festival and the attendant activity in the city have made a significant contribution to the successful bid for this trophy, which puts Glasgow where it certainly belongs, among the foremost cities of Europe - 1985 Athens, 1986 Florence, 1987 Amsterdam, 1988 Berlin, 1989 Paris, 1990 Glasgow.

FACTS AND FIGURES

1888

Opened   8 May 1888 by the Prince and Princess of Wales
Closed   10 November 1888
Site   Kelvingrove Park, approx. 60 acres
Architect James Sellars of Campbell Douglas and Sellars
Admission 1 shilling (Thurs. 2s 6d); children 6d; schools 2d; 21 tickets £1; season ticket 1 guinea
Attendance 5,748,379 (including attendants)
Profit   £41,700 (the figure published in 1890)

1901

Opened   2 May 1901 by the Duke and Duchess of Fife (Princess Louise)
Closed   9 November 1901
Site   Kelvingrove Park, 73 acres
Architect James Miller
Admission 1 shilling; under 14 6d; 21 tickets £1; season ticket 1 guinea
Attendance 11,497,220 (including attendants)
Profit   £39,000 (the figure published in 1905)

1911

Opened   3 May 1911 by The Duke and Duchess of Connaught
Closed   4 November 1911
Site   Kelvingrove Park, 62 acres
Architect R. J. Walker of Walker and Ramsay
Admission 1 shilling; under 16 6d; season ticket 15 shillings
Attendance 9,369,375
Profit   Approx. £20,000

1938

Opened   3 May 1938 by King George VI and Queen Elizabeth
Closed   29 October 1938
Site   Bellahouston Park, 175 acres
Architect Thomas S. Tait and numerous assistants
Admission 1 shilling; children 6d; season £1 5s 0d
Attendance 12,593,232
Loss   Approx. £128,000

1988

Opened   28 April 1988 by the Prince and Princess of Wales
Closed   26 September 1988
Site   Prince's Dock, approx. 120 acres
Architects Gillespie's (site designers and co-ordinators of the contributions of many architects)
Admission £5; 5-16 £2.50; family day ticket £13.50; season tickets £15 up to £45
Loss   The 'net cost' is estimated at £15 million

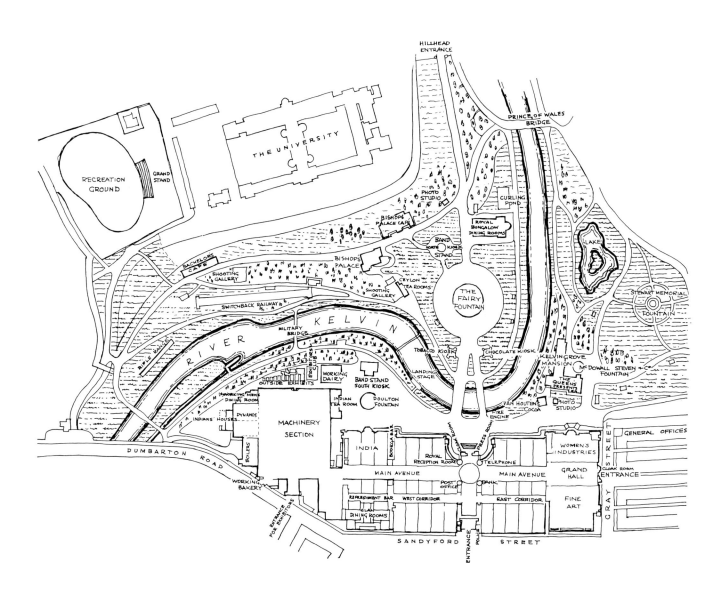

1. The International Exhibition, Glasgow, 1888, held in Kelvingrove Park. (Based on the official plan.)

1888

2. View north from the Main Building. The right-hand bridge dates from the Prince of Wales' last visit to Glasgow in 1868, to lay the foundation stone for the new University building shown here on the hill; the left-hand one was erected temporarily for the Exhibition. Flanking them are Howell's and Assafrey's 'kiosks' (the artist misread his sketch in labelling the latter), and on the far left is the reconstructed Bishop's Palace. (*ILN*)

'Manchester and Edinburgh may *try* it, but Glasgow can *do* it.' Spurred by civic rivalry, Glasgow launched its first major exhibition in an attempt to trump both the 1887 Royal Jubilee Exhibition held by Manchester, a major industrial competitor, and the 1886 International Exhibition of its old adversary Edinburgh. The Glasgow International Exhibition was to be the largest in Britain since the London show of 1862, and the Admissions Race was on.

Victorian Glasgow possessed all the main attributes of an exhibition city. On a great river, at the heart of an international trading network, it

Notes to this chapter appear on page 189.

17

B

was one of the world's leading manufacturing centres. In 1888 its population of 761,000 (or one and a half million including its district) made it easily Britain's second city, a title claimed since 1811. After an astonishingly rapid recovery from financial crisis in 1878, it had achieved a new industrial prosperity and confidence. Indeed since the eighteenth century Glasgow's entrepreneurs had shown a notable capacity for moving with the times, and countering set-backs by turning to new fields. Tobacco and sugar importers had made the first Glasgow fortunes. When these were lost in the American War of Independence, cotton became the basis for the city's rapid industrial expansion from the 1830s onwards. By the time the textile industry was in decline, chiefly because of the American Civil Wars, Glaswegian energies had already turned to the heavy industries built upon Lanarkshire's rich seams of coal and ironstone. With earlier interests not entirely extinguished, and other enterprises spawned by the major concerns (an enormous chemical industry, for example, grew from the bleachworks which serviced the textile factories), Glasgow in the closing decades of the nineteenth century showed a notable diversity of manufacturing industry, ranged round the central shipyards and steel-making works. Though the economy was subject to cyclical depression, and its industries dangerously inter-reliant and dependent upon foreign markets, manufacturers looked to the solidity of the achievement so far and the proven capacity of native engineers for technological innovation: they saw no cloud in a future of confident expansion.

Further assets were Glasgow's powerful civic pride and well-developed municipal mentality. At a period when there was virtually no involvement in the city's affairs by government in Westminster, political allegiance was first and foremost to the city. Within the limits of the social attitudes of the time, Glasgow's City Council was a model of its kind, taking an energetic view of its responsibility for the city's welfare. Indeed Glasgow was famous for its bold and successful experiments in municipalisation. Commendable headway had been made with the provision of public water, gas, trams, laundries, markets, hospitals and parks, and to some extent with slum clearance. The lasting blot on Glasgow's reputation, the dreadful housing and degrading poverty of the lowest classes, was inherent in the capitalist exploitation of labour that had brought prosperity to the city and the individuals who ran it. This was a problem too huge to be solved on the rates or by local charity. Besides which the belief was still available at this period that the misery of the 'unrespectable' poor was the consequence of fecklessness and moral turpitude. In the circumstances it is not surprising that the public building of this period aimed to enhance Glasgow's status as a great industrial power rather than to rehouse her poor. A permanent expression of this outlook was the magnificent Municipal Chambers, begun in 1883, and completed at the cost of half a million pounds to be opened by Queen Victoria in 1888. The City liked it to be recognised that such things were done on the grand scale.

Glasgow then was ready for a major exhibition, which can be seen in the context of this vigorous municipal activity as another bid for a cultural status to match the city's industrial strength. The general aims espoused in the prospectus were a mixture of the altruism and shrewd commercial instinct characteristic of Victorian exhibitions: 'to promote and foster Science and Art, by exciting the inventive genius of our people'; and 'to stimulate commercial enterprise by inviting all nations to exhibit their products both in the raw and finished state'. Pride and an obligation to match Edinburgh dictated that Glasgow's Exhibition should style itself 'international' in the tradition of the Great Exhibition of 1851.

More specifically, and again in emulation of the Crystal Palace, the Exhibition had been conceived - in the confident expectation of a profit - as a means of funding the new Art Gallery, Museum and School of Art which were seen as necessary to reflect the city's growing stature. Existing museum accommodation was inadequate and fragmented. The Fine Art collection, lately much enlarged by bequests from local magnates, had outgrown the McLellan Galleries acquired by the Corporation in 1856, and the building had furthermore proved a fire risk. In 1870 an Industrial Art collection had been started in the unsuitable setting of Kelvingrove Mansion, built in about 1783 for the Glasgow merchant Patrick Colquhoun. Even after its extension by public subscription in 1876 it could not accommodate the growing size and scope of the collection, which now included natural history and large pieces of industrial technology.

Plans to include a new School of Art were aimed at improving the standard of art and technical education in the city. (In the event the School was separately constructed, but close formal links with the Museum remained.) There had been a strong movement for design reform in Scotland since the late eighteenth century, and general interest in this issue grew in the decades after the Great Exhibition of 1851 and the consequent establishment of the South Kensington Museum and Art School. Manufacturers were becoming increasingly aware of the importance of design in production and marketing to a new middle class of consumers. The relationship between Art and Industry was a subject particularly dear to the heart of Francis (Fra) Newbery, the dynamic new Headmaster of the Glasgow School of Art and Haldane Academy, who had been appointed in 1885. He came imbued with the whole South Kensington philosophy and exhibition tradition, having taught there before his move to Glasgow, and it was under his leadership that the School's distinctive contribution in art, architecture and especially design developed towards the end of the century. His new curriculum was intended to offer 'a complete cycle of Technical Artistic Education applicable to the Industrial Arts of the city of Glasgow'. Education, art and industry were seen as an integrated whole which would serve society by increasing the general level of prosperity.[1] The ideology central to exhibitions was alive and flourishing in Glasgow.

There was of course a pressing unofficial aim - to surpass the efforts of Edinburgh and Manchester. Edinburgh was fairly easy game: for all its international pretensions 1886 had been a predominantly Scottish affair; indeed most of the important exhibitors there had been Glasgow firms, its

3 and 4. Preparations: retouching Sir John Steell's statue of Queen Victoria which sat in front of the Main Building; and delivering exhibits on temporary rails. (*Quiz*)

PRESIDENT
Sir ARCHIBALD C. CAMPBELL, of Blythswood,
Baronet, M.P.

CHAIRMAN
The Honourable Sir JAMES KING, of Campsie, LL.D.
Lord Provost of Glasgow.

THE PRESIDENT AND THE EXECUTIVE COUNCIL
OF THE
INTERNATIONAL EXHIBITION, GLASGOW, 1888,

Request the honour of your presence in the Grand Hall of the Exhibition on Tuesday, 8th May,
on the occasion of the
OPENING OF THE EXHIBITION
By T.R.H. the Prince and Princess of Wales.

27 ST. VINCENT PLACE,
GLASGOW, APRIL, 1888.

William M. Cunningham, Secy.

5. The invitation to the royal opening, with a panoramic view of the Exhibition: on the right is the University tower.

6. Work progressing on the Doulton Fountain, which was built from moulded terracotta bricks. (*Quiz*)

main building was designed by the Glasgow architect John Burnet, and the Corporation had contributed handsomely to the guarantee fund. Its General Manager, H. A. Hedley (who had run exhibitions in London in 1883-5), was appointed to the same post in Glasgow. The two Exhibitions had much in common, including Artisans' and Women's Industries sections; but Glasgow's was as necessary very much bigger and better. Manchester's acclaimed Jubilee Exhibition was a more serious rival, and Glasgow's was constantly compared with it, the palm being given now to one, now the other.

Competition faced by Glasgow's show in 1888 illustrates the popularity of exhibitions in this decade. In London one could choose from the Italian, Irish or Anglo-Danish Exhibitions. Abroad there were the Scandinavian Exhibition in Copenhagen, and, on the international level to which Glasgow aspired, big exhibitions in Brussels, Barcelona, and (later in the year) Melbourne. Though most customers for Glasgow's Exhibition came from the west of Scotland, it was important for the organisers' purpose to encourage tourism from further afield. The belief was as firm a century ago as today that 'Glasgow has only to be better known to become more popular'.[2] Excellent communications and the proximity of sublime and rugged scenery were stressed. At the practical level the relevant committee arranged package deals with the steamship companies and cheap excursions on the railways, which were encouraged to reduce the journey time from London to Glasgow to an impressive eight hours.

The Exhibition organisers, like the City Council, were drawn from Glasgow's business and professional élite. They had no problem with raising financial backing, something which had hindered many another such enterprise: the guarantee fund reached about £300,000. All arrange-

A Bit of Doulton

7. Opening day: the royal procession approaching the Hillhead entrance to the grounds beneath a triumphal arch. (*ILN*)

8. The Prince of Wales unlocked the Exhibition with a gold and enamel key. Mr John Chubb's Gothic design incorporated the Scottish lion and thistle leaves, and the arms of Glasgow with St Mungo. The wards of the key formed the initials GE. (*Official Guide*)

ments were executed with an effectiveness which reflected the city's commercial acumen. Work progressed fast on a site in Kelvingrove Park (laid out by Sir Joseph Paxton himself in 1853, the first and most picturesque of the three parks he designed for Glasgow). The city at large was spruced up, with roads remade, shop fronts painted, new uniforms for the tramway attendants. Preparations were on the whole complete by the time the Press was shown round. The newspaper men were well looked after and pronounced favourably on what they saw.

On 8 May 1888, a day of bright sunshine with a smart breeze to do justice to the countless flags and banners which decorated the city, the Prince and Princess of Wales drove through cheering crowds to the Exhibition. Here with a golden key the Prince unlocked the Main Building, a glittering 'Eastern Palace' overlooking the River Kelvin. The occasion was accounted a brilliant success, fully worthy of Scotland's greatest city. Edinburgh was put firmly in the shade.

The competition for the design of the Exhibition had been won by Glasgow architect James Sellars. He chose an Oriental style, he explained, 'not only from its suitability to the purpose, but because it lends itself readily to execution in wood'. His mish-mash of Byzantine, Moorish and Indian influences, soon dubbed 'Bagdad by Kelvinside', could not pretend to architectural distinction. But the vast domed Main Building, with its fretted towers and minarets, boldly striped in dark red and cream, and the picturesque minor buildings, pierced with horse-shoe arches, were thoroughly appropriate. They offered at comparatively low cost the desired novelty and contrast to the soot-stained sandstone of the city. Sellars' untimely death in October, allegedly from blood-poisoning after stepping on a nail at the Exhibition, came at the height of his renown.

The floor area of the Main Building (474,500 sq ft) was carefully calculated to exceed that of Manchester's. Its layout was that commonly seen in exhibition architecture - a great nave crossed by a transverse avenue, with a Grand Central Dome dominating the structure inside as well as out. A square annexe for Machinery in Motion was appended to the west end. The *Official Guide* lingers raptly over the 'gorgeous and striking' colouring of the interior: down the Main Avenue a frieze of stencilled red on gold, enriched with blue-green; in the Dome quaint arabesques of strong red, blue, yellow and green, and gilt iron work. The arches and coves of the Dome were painted with the scriptural texts and allegorical figures which were *de rigeur* in exhibition décor. The four ladies presiding on this occasion were painted by 'Glasgow Boys' James Guthrie, who did 'Art'; G. T. Henry, 'Industry'; Edward Walton, 'Agriculture'; and John Lavery, 'Science'. Above the figures were the armorial bearings of Britain, France, Germany and the USA, claiming an international range for the Exhibition which was not altogether justified by the exhibits to which visitors, having peered perhaps at the luxurious Royal Reception Room in the Dome's north west corner, would now proceed.

Many might have headed first to the Fine Art Section which had become a prestigious part of major exhibitions, and was particularly connected with the aims of this one. It occupied the south east end of the

9 (*opposite*). The Grand Entrance of the Main Building. The Dome (170 ft high including the vane) was covered in galvanised sheet iron on an iron framework, and the four octagonal towers flanking it were built of brick. The rest of the building was mostly of painted wood.

10. Off the main 'Moresque' Royal Reception Room were two retiring rooms and this dining room, all furnished and decorated by Wylie and Lochhead of Glasgow. The dark colouring and 'Scottish Baronial' oak furniture obeyed contemporary conventions in dining room décor. The furniture has recently returned to Kelvingrove from South Africa.

building and was brick-built and fire-proofed with a view to being retained as a temporary housing after the Exhibition. An enormous collection of 2700 exhibits was displayed in ten galleries - seven of painting
(both British and foreign, divided into loan and sale collections); and one
each of sculpture, architecture and photography. Commissions for murals
in the last three from Messrs Roche, Hornel, Nairn, and McGregor Wilson, together with the roundels in the Dome mentioned above, represented enlightened if long overdue patronage of the local 'Boys'. This was
valuable exposure for the talented group of rebellious young artists who,
largely unacknowledged at home, were already contributing to Glasgow's
strong artistic reputation in the outside world. The Exhibition undoubtedly assisted in turning some of them into established painters.[3]

11. Looking from the Dome down the Main
Avenue East. One can make out the stencilled
designs, drapes and banners which decorated
the interior. Behind Osler's display of cut glass
is the polar bear atop the Artic Tannery's stand.

12. Looking from the Dome down the Main Avenue West. The French Court is on the left. The skilled visual reporting of the *Illustrated London News* artist makes an interesting comparison with the century-old photograph on the opposite page.

While Manchester had mounted a fine show of fifty years of English painting, and Edinburgh had concentrated on the French and Dutch schools, Glasgow went for everything. Quality was consequently submerged by quantity. Most to popular taste were the numerous paintings of anecdotal, sentimental or heroic subjects by artists like Orchardson, Pettie, Faed or Robert Gibb, whose *Thin Red Line* drew the greatest crowds as well as much critical scorn. 'In truth,' opined *The Builder*, 'the crowd of picture-seers at Glasgow seemed to be even more hopelessly ignorant of the meaning of the painting and sculpture than the crowd at the Royal Academy, and that is saying a great deal.'[4] Nevertheless the loan collection included many indisputably fine things by recognised masters like Corot, Turner, Constable, and Gainsborough, as well as more recent painters. Here the committee had profitted from the notable collections of many local industrialists, like Sir Charles Tennant, of the great St Rollox chemical works; or James Reid, of the locomotive builders Neilson and Co., many of whose paintings were given to the City after his death. Other loans came from further afield: Rossetti's fine *Dream of Dante*, for example, was lent by the Corporation of Liverpool. This painting prompted a call from the critic of *Quiz* magazine for more municipal patronage of the arts in Glasgow; but it was not until 1891 that the

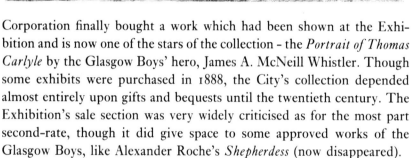

13 and 14. *The Thin Red Line* by Robert Gibb, showing a Highland regiment standing firm at Balaclava: one of the Exhibition's most popular pictures though far from its most distinguished. Its admirers included all echelons of society. (*AJ, Quiz*)

Corporation finally bought a work which had been shown at the Exhibition and is now one of the stars of the collection - the *Portrait of Thomas Carlyle* by the Glasgow Boys' hero, James A. McNeill Whistler. Though some exhibits were purchased in 1888, the City's collection depended almost entirely upon gifts and bequests until the twentieth century. The Exhibition's sale section was very widely criticised as for the most part second-rate, though it did give space to some approved works of the Glasgow Boys, like Alexander Roche's *Shepherdess* (now disappeared).

The sculpture section, of which Fra Newbery was convener, was more disciplined and successful, attempting a full display of fifty years of sculpture to rival Manchester's retrospective of painting. French and English work made up the bulk of the 170 exhibits. The collection was thought likely to be very educational, as the local tradition in sculpture was not strong at this period, though work by the young Kellock Brown attracted some notice. The architectural drawings section, reflecting the contemporary vitality of Glasgow's architectural profession, was judged by specialist critics to be remarkably good and one department in which Glasgow easily surpassed Manchester. A second corridor gallery was devoted to photography, another area in which Glasgow had a lively tradition, centering on the firm of T. & R. Annan, founded in 1855. J. C. Annan was responsible for the official photography of the Exhibition.

Industrial Art however was the main business of the building. Its exhibitors - not including Women, Artisans and Foreigners - were categorised into 21 classes, from Agriculture, Horticulture and Arboriculture, to Music and Musical Instruments. In between was a vast range of

15. The Gray Street entrance to the Main Building, showing the brick construction of the Fine Art Section to the left. (*ILN*)

16. The sculpture gallery was 150 ft long but only 26 ft wide. In the foreground is *The Last Call*, by C. B. Birch, a work similar in appeal to Gibb's *Thin Red Line* (opposite). (*ILN*)

industrial production, from pig-iron in Class 2 to lawn tennis outfits in 20, with nearly every department represented by a manufacturer from Glasgow or the environs. Some two thirds of the approximately 2000 exhibits came from Scotland.

All exhibitors saw a hard core of commercial advantage in their presence. At the Great Exhibition of 1851 price tags had been idealistically prohibited; in 1888 on the contrary the regulations asked that they be provided for information, though the sale for immediate removal of articles exhibited was forbidden. Goods produced in demonstrations were excepted from this ban, which was an incentive to the popular working displays. The Exhibition was invaluable for bringing goods before the

17. Brown and Poulson's corncob arches, advertising their famous cornflour and starch. Behind is the mustard stand of J. & J. Colman, another firm to survive as a household name.

18. The multifarious products of the Thistle Rubber Mills were shown with less pretension to artistry.

consumer's eye: Neilson, Shaw, Macgregor, for instance, turned over in their Glasgow shop large quantities of the tartan merchandise (including the Flora Macdonald tartan scarf, 'as worn in 1745') displayed in the Exhibition. The demonstration facility was very advantageous for items like Royle's Self-Pouring Teapot: orders could be placed provided they were supplied from outside. Private orders could be substantial, like that secured by Gardner's, the furnishing firm, from the visiting King of the Belgians. Important commercial transactions were also made. Post Office,

19 (*opposite*). Window dressing by Robin and Houston, who had soapworks at Paisley and candleworks in Glasgow. Glass jars display the 'Chemical Aspect of Soap Making'.

Bank and Telephone facilities centrally located under the Grand Dome were there to assist. Coverage of the Exhibition in the specialist, national and international press offered further valuable advertising.

Most stands in the Industrial Art section aimed at overwhelming the spectator with the sheer quantity and variety of goods displayed, but the more imaginative used virtuoso feats of skill to good effect: busts of Her Majesty done in soap, for instance, or the gigantic corncob arches marking Brown and Poulson's stand. Capturing the attention was everything in the fiercely competitive business of exhibiting. The Singer Company, with characteristic acumen, was running a draw for a family sewing machine

20. People of all classes attended the Exhibition. This cartoon alludes to leaks in the roof which appeared during storms in late May, and illustrates some ambitious carving in White Windsor soap from Margerison's of Preston: round a relief-carved tower were arranged the Laocoon group, and busts of the Queen, Prince Consort, Prince and Princess of Wales, Burns, Scott, Livingstone and President Garfield. (*Fun and Frolic*)

21. Country lad: 'Gie's a penny-worth o' thae sma' ceegaurs!' Young lady: 'Sorry I can't; only sell our cigarettes in boxes at 9d and 1/6.' The naiveté of rural visitors was a constant source of amusement in the press. (*Bailie*)

worth £10. Many manufacturers realised that a pretty attendant, especially one in fancy dress, did wonders for their sales: Muratti's tobacco girls, who uninterrupted could each turn out up to 2000 hand-made Turkish cigarettes a day, were particularly popular. Working exhibits were generally commercially successful as well as appropriately instructive: a loom in operation secured for R. W. Forsyth's 'hygienic woollen underwear', for example, a public which might otherwise have passed it by.

Displays by companies not directly oriented to the consumer were often genuinely educational, like the Earnock Colliery's full-size reproduction of a miner's work place equipped with the latest improvements (including electric lamps, the first in the UK), and complete with a rather charming but unrealistically dapper dummy collier, pick upraised to attack the face. The late Dr James 'Paraffin' Young was claimed with pride by Glasgow as the father of an important industry: Young's Paraffin Light and Mineral Co. illustrated his process for the distillation of Scottish bituminous shale into useful by-products. The Tharsis Sulphur and Copper Company exhibited a contour model of its Spanish mines and examples of the production process, from raw ores to a 36 cwt lump of pure copper, but attracted most attention with an uncatalogued afterthought - an archaeological display of Phoenician, Carthaginian and Roman material found in the ancient mines since their purchase in 1866.

A visitor progressing the length of the wide Main Avenue would pass exhibits of general appeal shown by many prestigious concerns. The far east end of the Avenue was partially shut off to form the Grand Hall, boldly decorated in red and yellow, with festoons of red and blue cloth and fringed heraldic trophies. Here concerts and daily organ recitals were held, under the eye of a colossal statue of Burns by Sir John Steell. The same artist had also executed an enormous Sir Walter Scott inside the main entrance. These were Glasgow's answer to Edinburgh's giant Wallace. Backing onto Burns, and making 'a fitting termination' to the Grand Hall, was the immense display of upholstery and carpets shown by James Templeton and Co., a major Glasgow employer and a vigorous representative of the wool industry which had persisted through the dramatic rise and decline of cotton in the area. (In the following year the firm moved to its magnificent new Glasgow Green factory, modelled on the Doges' Palace, and continued to expand well into the next century.) Costume and fabric displays in this part of the Hall underlined the fine quality of the locally surviving textile industry. Most striking were the white and gold cases of Copland and Lye, brilliant against the prevailing black of surrounding stands. Also eye-catching - gorgeous or garish according to taste - were the exhibits of Turkey Red dyeing by the three remaining Vale of Leven manufacturers. This industry had been revolutionised by the comparatively recent discovery of a substitute for natural madder derived from coal tar.

Trophies of cotton reels in various shapes erected by Clarks of Paisley were eclipsed by the large display of their rivals Coats, who put a good 50,000 spools of sewing thread into a model of their new spinning mill at Ferguslie. Electrically driven machines showing various processes added instruction to spectacle to enhance the firm's prestige. Next came a fine collection of products from the Arctic Tannery, Dundee, ornamented by heads of walrus, cariboo, etc., 'the whole being surmounted by a polar bear'. Osler's of London and Birmingham were prominent with a lavish display of cut glass, which was coming into fashion again, to the disapproval of some champions of taste.

Taking first place on the western side of the Grand Dome was the art wares stand of Doulton and Co. of Lambeth, who were present in force at the Exhibition, as they had been at Manchester and elsewhere. Like the other manufacturers of bronze, pottery and glass art ware located nearby, Doulton's was the sort of firm which profitted straightforwardly from using the Exhibition as a huge shop-window. There was a tendency to accretion of exhibits in this category as the Exhibition ran on: 'a ton or two of this class of goods might be carted away' commented one observer.

From these crammed stalls the visitor passed to one of the Exhibition's outstanding features, the exquisitely executed ship models of the extensive Naval Architecture and Marine Engineering Department. Here Glasgow's chief industrial glory was given glamorous prominence. Tyneside was represented, but was naturally somewhat overwhelmed by the famous local names. At this period there were close on 40 separate yards on the Clyde, and nearly all the builders of note, along with some of the big ship-owners, were exhibiting. The largest array of ship models ever seen portrayed the diversity of the Clyde's shipbuilding achievement - millionaires' pleasure boats, luxury liners, ironclads, cargo ships. Fairfield for example included the *Livadia*, the fantastic steam yacht built for the Czar in 1880, and a design for the proposed new Guion liner capable of a five day crossing from the Clyde to New York (this was not in fact achieved within the century); J. and G. Thomson exhibited the much

22. Fairfield's large stand on the Main Avenue. The firm, formed in 1886 from the Elders' business at Govan, was showing about 30 ship models along with a model of a triple expansion engine. Rails, packing cases and scuffed woodwork indicate that the photograph was taken at the end of the Exhibition.

23. The lavishly carved and painted dining saloon of the two-storey deck house erected by Wm Denny and Bros of Dumbarton.

24. Doulton's 'Indian Pavilion' at the west end of the Main Avenue, flamboyantly in keeping with the Oriental architectural style of the Exhibition. Pots thrown, fired and decorated within were sold as souvenirs. More ship models can be seen at the side of the Avenue.

admired *City of New York*, built for the Inman Line, the largest mercantile steamship afloat; Napier's, the 'kindergarten' of so many renowned marine engineers, showed equal numbers of naval and merchant vessels; Lobnitz and Co. displayed the dredger *Dérocheuse*, recently built for the Suez Canal Company.

In the last decades of the Victorian era competition in the improvement of steamships and in the increasingly efficient harnessing of steam power was intense – with Germany and the USA, and with other British yards – but Clydeside kept its place in the vanguard thanks to the famous excellence of Scottish engineers. A number of firms showed models of the triple expansion engines developed by Dr A. C. Kirk of Napier's (some of these were in the Machinery Section), but Wm Denny and Bros of Dumbarton went one further with Walter Brock's patent design for a quadruple expansion engine, a model alleged to have cost £1300, an enormous sum at this period. But Denny's really stole the show with what was one of the sights of the Exhibition, a spectacular first class deck-house – a dining

C

saloon and a lady's stateroom (decorated with Japanese embroideries and neatly convertible to a sitting-room), with a handsome stair to music and smoke rooms above. Everything was richly embellished in conventional taste. All the work had been executed by the decorative department of the Leven yard, underlining the quality of the local ship-building industry and its importance as a stimulus to many other trades. The cost of this exhibit was put at 'fully £5000'. The Allan Line's example of intermediate accommodation on one of its ships was more modest but still very appealing to the public.

Emerging impressed from this section, the visitor could have paused to watch twelve men at work behind glass on the stand of the London Diamond Cutting Company, which had been set up in 1871 to revive the skill of diamond cutting in Britain. (The gems dealt with were locked up at night on the Transverse Avenue in Chubb's replica of the gilded steel cage made to protect the Koh-i-noor diamond in 1851.) Lastly came the most conspicuous exhibit in this area, Doulton's Indian Pavilion. Within this impressive structure of glazed and enamelled terracotta skilled hands were at work on all the processes of pot-making. Like other demonstration displays this fed an avid demand for souvenirs, besides being fascinating to the public. The firm had a third exhibit in the sanitary section, and had also supplied all the Exhibition's lavatory fittings and tiling in their latest designs. Their substantial showing was completed in the grandest style with the Doulton Fountain outside the building, a gift to the City of Glasgow. Designed by A. C. Pearce, and claimed as the largest such structure executed in terracotta, it gave expression to the untroubled imperial attitudes seen elsewhere in the Exhibition: four pairs of figures representing India, Canada, South Africa and Australia were surmounted by a tier of three soldiers and a sailor, and on top of all (above another tier of unspecific water-pourers), the Queen with orb and sceptre. After the Exhibition the fountain was moved, following a year's argument about its relocation, to Glasgow Green, where, vandalised and in a sad state of disrepair, it still stands.

It was in fact the Empire, which of course did not really count, which provided most of the 'international' colour of the Exhibition. While the generous might regard the third of exhibits which came from beyond Scotland as 'a very liberal proportion', this included contributions from south of the border, which amounted to about one fifth of the whole - most from London, followed by Lancashire, then Yorkshire and Newcastle. The less indulgent insisted that this 'so called "International Exhibition" is not really international except in so far that foreign exhibits have been invited, and that some few are to be seen here and there'.[5] The genuinely foreign section, numbering about 70 exhibitors, was indeed thin and miscellaneous: a few American firms, assorted French, Germans and Italians, porcelain and glass from Vienna and Bohemia, Heineken's lager from Amsterdam, maraschino from Dalmatia, three Australian wine importers who did not fit in elsewhere, and a Danish firm touting 'Albumen Maltose', a new health food. Nations were by now well geared to squab-

25. The grandly imperial Doulton Fountain which stood outside the Main Building. Its battered remains are now on Glasgow Green. (*Pen-and-Ink Notes*)

26. Viennese bric-a-brac from Ernest Wahliss, typical of the consumer-oriented displays of the small foreign section. More Bohemian 'art porcelain' is visible at the side.

bling for space at major international fairs: it was clear that they did not take Glasgow seriously enough to feel the need to protect prestige by appearing officially at this Exhibition.

Contributions from the Empire could be more easily drummed up. Pride of place went to India, reflecting Glasgow's strong trading connections with that country, as well as the general hankering for the exotic visible in the Oriental architectural style of the Exhibition. Considerable trouble was taken to ensure a good display, with committees in Calcutta, Bombay and Madras, a visit to Glasgow by Mr Mukharji, who had represented India at the London Colonial and Indian Exhibition of 1886, and a substantial sum allocated for the purchase of exhibits in India. Goods were carried home free of charge by City, Anchor and Clan Line steamers. The result was a rich bazaar of art wares, fabrics, carpeting, carved furniture and curiosities, catering to the European consumer's conception of

India. There was plenty of added colour: 'In a recess a Brahmin fakir is seen doing penance on a spiked bed', says the *Guide* tantalisingly.

Most appealing was the 'Indian Street' set up in the corridor, where native artisans (who were housed by the dynamo shed) plied their trades and supplied souvenirs of jewellery, pottery, carved work and sweetmeats. Such disguised 'human exhibits' (the people being more interesting than the crafts they practised) had become a standard attraction at exhibitions, but this did not dim the fascination for Glaswegians of being able to examine at close quarters some of the more exotic subjects of their Empire. This was the attraction also of being served by native waiters on the verandah of the Royal Bungalow, or in the Indian or Ceylon tea rooms - a little taste of the imperial way of life. Glasgow at this period was racially homogenous, apart from its Irish and Jewish immigrant communities, and people were not exposed to convincing images of foreigners: exhibitions were a valuable source of information now freely available in other forms. The 'experience' offered was of course completely controlled by the exhibiting power, in the case of the subject peoples shown. Ceylon's main exhibit, and its popular tea house in Kandyan style, for instance, were designed by J. G. Smithers, late architect to the Ceylon Government.

27. Australian Wine Importers Ltd, trying to break into the Scottish market with 'The Honest Products of our Kinsmen'. Cheapness was a further recommendation: clarets from 1s 4d, champagne 4s a quart. (*Pictorial World*)

28 and 29. Artisans in the popular 'Indian Street'. (*Quiz, ILN*)

The white dominion of Canada exhibited on an altogether different footing. Its government was actively recruiting new Canadians and took space to mount a display of resources, cities and scenery for the information of 'intending emigrants, capitalists, investors and tourists'. The Exhibition provided a very useful channel of communication for such specific aims. Emigration reached its nineteenth-century peak in the 1880s: thousands of Scots were abandoning their homeland every year and Canada was their favourite destination. Australia surprisingly was not seriously represented at the Exhibition. Antipodean interest was presumably focussed on the Melbourne Exhibition which opened in September.

One of the most genuinely international parts of the Exhibition was in fact the large Women's Art and Industries section. This was a tribute to the energies of the unemployed females of the aristocratic and upper middle classes who organised it very much as their own show. The Honorary Council was stiff with Duchesses, Countesses, Marchionesses and assorted Ladies, and 'connections' had been effective in assembling a large array of foreign material alongside the displays in the English and Welsh, Irish and Scottish courts. The Empress of Germany (Britain's Princess

30. The bazaar-like display of the Indian Court, with attendants. The sign proclaims the gift of the Tower of Silence, an elaborate carved 'temple', to Kelvingrove Museum - where it still lies in store. Other Indian material was purchased for the City's collection.

Royal) had arranged exhibits from German elementary and technical schools; and cases of material had come from Madeira, Russia, Greece, Jamaica, Montreal, Iceland and many other places. Royal patronage was concrete here: there were cushions from the Empress and the Crown Princess of Denmark; Princess Christian of Schleswig-Holstein put in a burnt-leatherwork chair and Princess Louise a terracotta plaque. 'Many of the lady visitors to the Exhibition may feel anxious to get to this section before troubling themselves about anything else', thought the *Official Guide*. There was a nice air of feminine solidarity about this corner of the show.

Here it was particularly evident that while the Exhibition as a whole did genuinely appeal to all sectors of society, the attitudes and interests pervading it were those of the classes profiting from the industrial boom. The Women's Section was segregated at the 'genteel' end of the Exhibition, next to the Grand Hall, in a way that reflected the rigid distinctions in middle-class society between the rôles of men and women. Following the lead of the Edinburgh Exhibition however the organisers adopted the serious aim of promoting opportunities of gainful employment for

1888

31. Mrs Eliot exhibiting wood-carving in the Women's Section. The Ladies' Committee was aiming to promote commercial craftwork of this sort as a respectable occupation for middle-class women.

32. The Hon. Secretary, Miss Meta Macdonald, looking fashionable, feminine and efficient. (*Pen-and-Ink Notes*)

33 (*opposite*). At the entrance to the Machinery Court was the magnificent ornamental ironwork of Walter Macfarlane's Saracen Foundry at Possilpark. Macfarlane's was a frequent medal-winner at international exhibitions, and its products were distributed all over the world in the late Victorian and Edwardian periods.

women, particularly 'educated' women, displaying work in fields like typewriting, wood engraving and other crafts which were now respectably open to them. Exhibited in this connection were designs for curtains, wall-hangings and carpets. *Not* represented were the thousands of poor women who minded the machines in the textile factories and many other industries, and who along with children provided the employers with their cheapest and most easily exploited labour.

The emphasis throughout was on the attractive home industries. While the Prince of Wales was in the Machinery Court observing mechanised lace-making on the Nottingham system (recently set up in Ayrshire as a Scottish challenge to the traditional Midlands industry), his consort was admiring the work of quaintly dressed traditional lace-makers in the Women's Section. There were also Shetland and Fairisle knitters, a Harris

tweed weaver, and a Tarbolton silk weaver. There was of course a large amount of fine needlework on display. The need to attack amateurishness and promote education in traditional fields of feminine labour was recognised in the prominence given to the display of the Royal School of Art Needlework, South Kensington, founded in 1872. It had erected a pretty room in Elizabethan style. The Glasgow School of Cookery tea room meanwhile was a popular resort for refreshment. Commercial industries demonstrated in this section included corset, glove, brush and artificial flower making, perfume manufacturing, Italian straw plaiting, and pottery; many others exhibited. But Eliza Tinsley and Co. of Dudley, manufacturer of small nails and chains, stands out as a lone example of such a firm apparently owned and run by a woman.

At the opposite end of the building was the man's world of Machinery in Motion. For many this throbbing, thundering display was 'undoubtedly the great feature of the Exhibition'. It could justly claim to be the best since the London show of 1862, indeed the best ever seen. The Machinery Section was central to the Victorian industrial exhibition: nothing more clearly enshrined the general belief in man's capacity for continuing progress in control of the world's resources. And here were represented in their most exhilarating form the engineering skills which supported Glasgow's present prosperity. The heart-stirring effect of all these whirling wheels and pistons is recorded in many places. 'It makes us proud of our country and its inventive genius that has done so much to increase the possibilities of life.'[6]

34. One of the many popular working displays in the Machinery Court: comfit-making. This sketch shows visitors looking down from the gallery. (*Pen-and-Ink Notes*)

This 'gigantic Workshop' appended to the Main Building was most impressive viewed from the wide gallery running round its sides. Its 160,000 sq ft of unimpeded exhibition space had been constructed and filled with the aid of an overhead travelling crane of 20 tons lifting power, which remained as a mighty exhibit. Glaswegians were proud of the grand scale of their products, and might have been disappointed to discover that because of pressure on space, the marine engines with which outsiders especially associated the city were not fully represented, while railway locomotives were conspicuous by their absence (except for scattered parts, and five machines used in construction shown by Sharp, Stewart and Co.) Interested visitors were assured of a courteous reception at the yards themselves.

Close on 350 exhibitors had however secured space, showing a great variety of industries, in which local firms again dominated the floor. Other manufacturing centres nevertheless mounted some spirited competition, for major producers now had to show at these large exhibitions in order to maintain their selling power. There was however little that was indisputably new. So while it is questionable how far the Exhibition achieved the noble aim of stimulating industrial progress in the absence of Britain's main competitors, Germany and the USA, it is certain that it provided a useful service for manufacturers shopping for up-to-date equipment, and in this pragmatic way assisted efficiency. Big business was done at the stands. Among notable challengers to the local eminences were Hawthorn,

35. The exhibit of Scott's Midlothian Oats, with female workers and a sales point. Machinery was driven from overhead shafting. (*Pictorial World*)

Leslie and Co. of Newcastle, with their model of a set of triple expansion engines for the Italian armour-clad *Sardegna*, claiming at 25,000 hp to deliver the largest power hitherto put into a vessel.

'The row is abominable, and so is the smell', was the reaction of a few visitors unsympathetic to heavy machines. Some exhibits in the Court did have more general appeal, like the Working Bakery run by Robert Thomson and Son of Crossmyloof, with several machines in operation, including a Power Drop Biscuit Machine and a continuous bread-baking oven. This was an awe-inspiring sight, and a popular source of snacks. Not every display was in motion: the Steel Company of Scotland, an important representative of the great expansion in local steel-making in the 1880s, achieved spectacle through height with a 'temple' of steel, while Hadfield's Steel Foundry, of Sheffield, chose overwhelming quantity, showing about 50 tons of assorted steel castings.

Power, like size and statistics, fascinated the Victorians. In the Boiler House and Dynamo Shed, large recesses in the Machinery Court, visitors could feel thrillingly close to visible and invisible energy. The steam from nine boilers was distributed by 2500 ft of piping, and four engines drove shafting to power the machinery in motion. A dozen different types of steam engine drove dynamos which supplied the new magic of electricity, deployed here on a scale claimed to surpass any previous. Electric light was indeed one of the most marvellous features of the Exhibition, symbolising progress in a spectacular manner. St Enoch Station and the Head Post Office in Glasgow were electrically lit back in 1879, but the novelty was slow to achieve general use. It was three years after the Exhibition that the Corporation established its first generating station. Electric street lighting was introduced in Glasgow in 1893.

The electric lighting contract for the Exhibition was apportioned three ways, the largest share going to the Anglo-American Brush Electric Light Company, who lit the grounds, most of the Main Building and the Machinery Court, using 18 miles of electric cables and 23 dynamos. The Thomson-Houston System, operated by a Glasgow contractor with 3 arc-light dynamos, was used in the Fine Art Gallery, and King, Brown and Co. of Edinburgh lit the first-class refreshment rooms with 750 incandescent Edison-Swan lamps in tulip-shaped shades of amber and ruby. In addition many stands were privately supplied with lighting by these com-

36. 'Trophies' of boiler tubing in the Machinery Section had their own chaste beauty. This is the exhibit of A. and J. Stewart's Clyde Tube Works at Coatbridge.

panies and other exhibitors of electric lighting plant, at a cost of 30 shillings a lamp for the duration of the Exhibition. These different systems could also be compared with the older illuminants: the latest gas and oil appliances were installed in other refreshment rooms and various lavatories. All this was properly in keeping with one of a Victorian exhibition's fundamental aims, to allow the informed assessment of rival products.

But easily the most spectacular application of electricity was outside, across the river, in the illuminated Fairy Fountain. After sundown it was the undisputed star of the whole show, and became one of the Exhibition's best loved features. Built by W. and J. Galloway of Manchester, earlier

37. The elegant display of George Cradock of Wakefield, manufacturer of Lang's Patent Steel Wire. Samples, new and worn, could be compared with conventional wire rope.

versions had attracted attention at South Kensington in 1886 and Manchester in 1887; but with its 120 ft diameter basin and quarter of a million candlepower, Glasgow's was confidently stated to excel anything of the kind previously seen. 'Electric rays' from 18 arc lights passed through slides of coloured glass to impinge upon a hundred jets of water, some rising to 150 ft. 'Magical effects', or more quaintly 'numberless dancing molehills of varied rainbow tints and exquisite beauty', were controlled by an operator in an adjacent tower. Beneath him in the engine room the powerful dynamos which drove the display could be inspected, to satisfy the urge for instruction.

The River Kelvin itself, winding through the grounds in its wooded glen, not only contributed picturesquely to the general scene, but had been cleaned and deepened for £1121 to enable its better use. On the sportive side there were rides in steam or electric launches, or especially popular, on a gondola imported from Venice and manned by a pair of 'real live gondoliers' (known locally as 'Signor Hokey' and 'Signor Pokey'). In the summer months however the river remained a great deal less appealing to the nose than to the eye, although the routine drainage into it of west Glasgow's sewage had been stopped for the Exhibition. Those bold enough to take part in the summer swimming galas had to be well hosed down afterwards. The 'Seweries' was wittily proposed as a substitute for the Exhibition's popular name, the 'Groveries'. While little use was made of the river for more serious purposes, apart from demonstrations of a self-righting lifeboat, it was nominated as an 'impromptu exhibit' in the cause of progress towards solving the problems of river pollution. This notion was in keeping with exhibition ideals, but doubtless unwelcome to the Executive - as was perhaps the horrifying display in the Main Building, by Peter Spence and Sons of Manchester, of samples of Clyde water and liquid Glasgow sewage before and after treatment with their chemicals. The city did in fact establish one of the first sewage farms in Britain in 1894.

38. The electrically illuminated Fairy Fountain, its brilliant effects reflected in the river. (*Quiz*)

39. The 'not very pellucid' Kelvin was used for swimming galas and water-sports. Also shown here are the Venetian gondola and a steam launch. On the bank is the Royal Bungalow restaurant: the insets advertise its wine list and imperial ambience. (*Fun and Frolic*)

There was still plenty to see outside the Main Building. Near at hand, in the old Kelvingrove Mansion Museum, were displayed 'in all probability' for the last time, as the advertisements proclaimed, the Queen's Jubilee presents, which had not previously been seen outside London. This motley treasure of 800 exhibits ranging from battle-axes to slippers had been notionally insured by the Corporation for £150,000 and was a

40 and 41. Glasgow's long-gone Bishop's Palace was impressively reconstructed. The cartoon alludes to public fascination with its realistic finish, and turns on one of the puns beloved of the period. Policemen were much in evidence at the Exhibition, to begin with at least, for fear of petty crime and rowdyism. (*ILN*, *Quiz*)

crowd-pulling coup for the Executive. Most of Her Majesty's loyal subjects found it deeply fascinating to view these tributes from all continents and all stations in life - from Birkenhead to Timbuctoo, from crowned heads to children of the Ragged Schools. The display overall reinforced the imperial flavour of the main Exhibition. Particularly sumptuous were the lavish gifts from Indian princes. But scores of silver caskets and illuminated loyal addresses lent special interest to exhibits like the model of the jubilee cake, which had weighed about a quarter of a ton.

The most important display outside the main building was on the University side of the river. Enjoying a certain romantic solitude, separated from the main Exhibition's concern with present and future, was a reproduction of the fifteenth-century Bishop's Palace or Castle which had once stood near Glasgow Cathedral. This had been reconstructed by Sellars from contemporary drawings: the original had been cleared away in 1792 to make way for the Royal Infirmary. Full scale 'Old Towns' had been popular features at Edinburgh and Manchester. This lonely representative of old Glasgow, of which so little now survived, soon became a prime attraction. It suffered badly from people poking it with their umbrellas, wondering what it was made of. The answer was canvas, on a wooden frame, painted extremely realistically.

Inside the Palace the embossed 'Tynecastle Canvas' wall-hanging developed by the Edinburgh decorator William Scott Morton was impressively deployed in the Bishop's Parlour. Some of Glasgow's notable artists in stained glass also contributed to good effect: J. and W. Guthrie and McCulloch and Gow each decorated rooms. In these atmospheric surroundings were housed archaeological and historical relics 'in a wealth and profusion never before achieved, and destined perhaps never to be repeated'.[7] There were 1546 lots in all, ranging from prehistoric bones to what was claimed as the first genuine crank-action bicycle, a cumbrous wooden machine made near Glasgow approximately fifty years previously. The magnitude of the collection caused a delay in opening. Unfortunately the Castle's inconvenient medieval conception and poor lighting and ventilation made it an inappropriate museum. It was simply too popular: 'Many visitors after crushing in are forthwith constrained simply to crush out again.'

No one could absorb the educational riches of the Exhibition without breaks for strolling in the grounds (which were charming with 'islet-lake, winding walks, gorgeous flowering plots, and splashing fountains') or taking recreational refreshment. There was a wide range of establishments to choose from, though class distinctions were sufficiently apparent to select the clientele. Jenkins Temperance Refreshment Rooms, straightforwardly identified as 'Working Men's Dining-Rooms' on the Exhibition plan, were tucked in between the Dynamo Shed and the Machinery Court, while the genteel Royal Bungalow occupied a prime position overlooking river, bandstand and the Fairy Fountain. There was a Bachelor's Café by the shooting range for those who preferred a 'men-only' ambience.

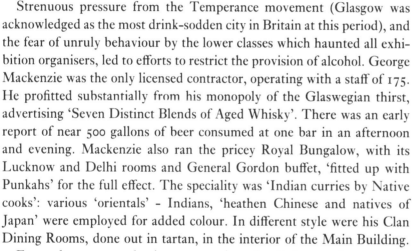

Strenuous pressure from the Temperance movement (Glasgow was acknowledged as the most drink-sodden city in Britain at this period), and the fear of unruly behaviour by the lower classes which haunted all exhibition organisers, led to efforts to restrict the provision of alcohol. George Mackenzie was the only licensed contractor, operating with a staff of 175. He profitted substantially from his monopoly of the Glaswegian thirst, advertising 'Seven Distinct Blends of Aged Whisky'. There was an early report of near 500 gallons of beer consumed at one bar in an afternoon and evening. Mackenzie also ran the pricey Royal Bungalow, with its Lucknow and Delhi rooms and General Gordon buffet, 'fitted up with Punkahs' for the full effect. The speciality was 'Indian curries by Native cooks': various 'orientals' - Indians, 'heathen Chinese and natives of Japan' were employed for added colour. In different style were his Clan Dining Rooms, done out in tartan, in the interior of the Main Building.

Fancy dress was a pleasing aspect of nearly all the catering arrangements. The contract for the large Bishop's Palace Temperance Café was secured by J. Lyons and Co., whose staff of 170 included ranks of waitresses in Mary Queen of Scots rig, nick-named 'Lyons' Widows'. The firm had operated successfully at the Newcastle Exhibition the year before, and it used the profits from Glasgow to establish its famous chain of London tea shops. The Indian and the Ceylon tea rooms, with verandahs and native waiters, also offered non-alcoholic refreshment. Van Houten's had brought over a complete Dutch cocoa house in sixteenth-century style, and fought successfully with the tea rooms for custom, urging that cocoa was nutritious, and cheaper and more satisfying than tea. Another alternative was offered by the 'scientific' milkmaids at the Working Dairy (where reposed as a further attraction Lipton's giant 5684 lb Canadian cheese). Also popular and ornamental were the two

42 (*left*). The Bodega Bar in the Main Building. Despite pressure from the Temperance movement for restrictions on the sale of alcohol large quantities were consumed.

43 (*above*). A waitress at J. Lyons' Bishop's Palace Temperance Restaurant, becomingly dressed in Mary Queen of Scots costume.

44. Van Houten's dark red sixteenth-century style Cocoa House was built by Dutch workmen and furnished inside with genuine antiques. Girls in national dress served cocoa at 2d a cup.

45. The switchback, the best loved feature of the Exhibition. Attendants were stationed below to pick up articles lost in the excitement. (*Quiz*)

oriental kiosks flanking the main bridge: Mr Assafrey provided chocolate, bon-bons and ices, Mr Howell catered for the smoker.

It was without doubt the amusements, segregated from the serious part of the Exhibition on the University side of the river, which secured its popular success. An unusual and nicely Scottish idea was the summer curling pond (the irons skimmed on castors over an asphalt rink). Here the winter pastime of curling could be simulated by enthusiasts, but in the exceptionally good summer weather the enterprising lessee was not very busy. The switchback railway on the other hand had become so commonplace that it was by now attracting the epithet 'inevitable' in accounts of exhibitions. But it was breathtakingly new to fun-starved Glaswegians and hugely popular. It became the most affectionately remembered feature of the Exhibition, the subject of many anecdotes about courting couples and country folk.

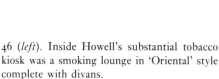

46 (*left*). Inside Howell's substantial tobacco kiosk was a smoking lounge in 'Oriental' style complete with divans.

47 and 48. The Exhibition's amusements included ascents in the captive balloon of Signor Balleni (who came from Warwickshire). His balloon was advertising Waterbury watches. Cycle-racing was one of the most popular sports of this period. (*Bailie, Quiz*)

Other attractions were also exhibition regulars: a captive air balloon, a military rifle range and a shooting gallery. This last was so successful that it was enlarged, and a second, an 'Indian jungle', erected in June. Sport was popular entertainment, and a series of events, including football matches, highland games and military tournaments, took place in the University Athletics Ground. The daily programme of music in the Grand Hall and grounds featured British and Continental bands - such as the Black Dyke Band, the Blue Hungarians and the Belgian Guides - as well as novelties like a band of harps from Birmingham. Music was one of the Exhibition's major outlays: the specially formed Exhibition Band under the improbably named Mr de Banzie cost £157 a week, and was judged good for the money (with a prodigious boy clarinetist); guest attractions like the Royal Artillery Band rated about £400 plus expenses. But these performances were credited with a 'considerable influence in disseminating a taste for music throughout a large part of the community'.[8] The grand finale came at the end of October with a band contest which drew over forty bands to Glasgow.

It is hard to imagine the impression made by this Exhibition, 'where the sun shines all day and the electric all night',[9] on a population which for the most part had never seen anything like it. 'By day, with bands playing and well-dressed crowds of promenaders, the scene is one of gaiety and brightness, and when night falls, and the electric light shines brilliantly, and from the fairy fountain the many-coloured waters climb into the sky, the sober-sided citizens of Glasgow can hardly believe that some spirit of enchantment has not transformed their own grey, steady-going town into the likeness of Paris on a fête day.'[10]

This intoxicating cosmopolitan atmosphere was greatly enhanced by the stream of tourists attracted to Glasgow. There was an influx of American visitors (and rain) as early as the end of May, and the exciting flow of 'foreigners', an exhibition in themselves, increased as the summer wore on, leading to severe pressure on hotel accommodation. The unofficial exhibition guides devoted considerable space to regional tourist attractions, urging cruises, Temperance hotels, and hydropathics as adjuncts to

49. The Clyde steamers did good business, among them the *Lord of the Isles*, a new paddle-steamer operated by the Glasgow and Inverary Steam-boat Company. Colourful and peculiar 'foreigners' were a source of fascination to locals.

50. Summer resorts lost some of their traditional business through Glaswegians' addiction to the Exhibition, but they compensated by attracting tourists brought to Scotland. (*Official Guide*)

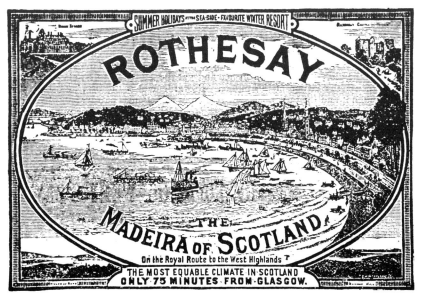

D

fine scenery. Glasgow shops were awash with souvenirs, supplementing the limited provision of the Exhibition itself; many of them, cheap transfer-printed ware, were in fact imported from Germany, where production costs were lower.

The discovery of the romantic Highlands by Queen Victoria and her beloved Albert had done more than anything to make Scotland a popular holiday destination. The Exhibition was given another lease of life and renewed coverage in the press when the Queen herself visited in state on 22 August on her way to Balmoral. Preparations were on the grand scale: there was a general flurry of repainting, a massive ornate porch was added

51. A panorama of the site, showing the full extent of the Main Building, and the Machinery Court with its smoking chimney. Kelvingrove Mansion can be seen on the left. In the foreground is the Royal Bungalow restaurant with the Fairy Fountain beyond; on the hill to the right the Bishop's Palace, with the Bishop's Palace Restaurant beside it. (*ILN*)

to the Main Building, new drapes of blue were introduced within, and Robert Burns was removed from the Grand Hall to make way for a throne. Glasgow itself was decorated to the hilt, and thousands lined the streets.

The Queen had only once before visited the city, in 1849. She was appalled by the slums, found the weather grim, and is reported to have said as she left that she disliked Glasgow and never wanted to go there again: certainly she managed to skirt the city when opening its Loch Katrine water supply in 1859. Glasgow *en fête* under miraculously sunny skies reversed some of these prejudices; and any Great Exhibition commended itself as a memorial to the achievements of her pined-for Consort.

GRAND HOTEL.
The Race for Hotels & Lodging Houses
at Railway Stations is something appalling.
But some Hotel Keepers are quite equal to
the occasion and fit up their Banqueting Halls
like STATE-ROOMS.

52. The Exhibition filled Glasgow with visitors, with resulting pressure on hotel accommodation. (*Fun and Frolic*)

The Queen visited again privately two days later and showed appropriate interest in the Women's and Indian Sections. For the municipal élite who hankered for the seal of royal approval and the recognition it entailed, the state visit was the triumph of the decade, if not the century. John Lavery was commissioned for £600 to record it on a vast canvas, over 8 x 13 ft (now in the Kelvingrove Art Gallery). 253 individuals required to be recognisable, and the many sittings this entailed, from the Queen downwards, established Lavery as a society portraitist. Glasgow did not see Victoria again but the City and the Exhibition had been given a major boost.

It was a grand show. Sophisticated outsiders were generally quite impressed, country visitors gaped open-mouthed, and Glaswegians simply loved it. Romance was in the air: young men were in love with pretty attendants and milkmaids at the Dairy. The press was full of Exhibition anecdotes, Exhibition doggerel, and dreadful Exhibition puns (e.g. 'young folks' season: the June-iors'). It was too much for some: 'People seem to have gone mad over the exhibition. Every brainless fool you meet asks you what you think of the Exhibition ... I think all exhibitions of this sort are the most infernal pieces of nonsense ever invented, and the Glasgow one is the worst of all.' There was some pick-pocketing and cheating on season-tickets, but for the most part the populace rose to exhortations in the press to good behaviour. Pride, fireworks and oriental splendour were a heady mixture, and Glasgow's loyal citizens committed themselves to making the Exhibition a success.

The lengths to which some were taking this became notorious. Figures comparing attendance with Edinburgh and Manchester had been published from the earliest days. As the summer turned autumnal the Admissions Race entered the final straight: Edinburgh's modest 2.5 million

TAKE IT EASY BOYS!
TAKE IT EASY,
WE HAVE STILL A MONTH AND A HALF
TO BREAK THAT MANCHESTER RECORD
· 4765137 ·

53. The Race to overtake the admissions total of Manchester's Jubilee Exhibition: according to the *Builder* 'this not very elevated order of emulation has been most diligently afoot for weeks, and certain active, long-limbed season-ticket men brag proudly, if somewhat sillily, of having done their stated dozens of admissions daily, over a considerable period'. This cartoon shows the Sandyford Street entrance to the Main Building, with Sir Walter Scott presiding. (*Fun and Frolic*)

had long been left in the rear, and sights were now set on Manchester or even London's 'Colinderies' (Colonial and Indian Exhibition) of 1886. As critics observed, it was misleading to roll attendants, complimentary and season ticket admissions into an overall total, though this was general practice; what really counted was payment of single admissions, and in this Manchester still had the lead in October. But season tickets were the key to the all-important grand total, as explained by this 'Glesca chappie' in *The Bailie*: 'Weel, boys, I think I'm daein' first-rate wi' the Exhibition. I've a season ticket, so I gang in at Gray Street, an' oot at Sandyford Street, then back an' oot an' back an' oot half-a-dizzen times a nicht. That's the way to bring up the attendance. Every oot an' in coonts, ye ken. If a' the season ticket folk wid dae like me we wid sune bring Glesca abune Manchester, aye, or London either.'[11] Manchester's 4,765,137 was overtaken, then with a final spurt London's 5,550,749. Glasgow squeezed home with 5,748,379. If some were ashamed of the dubious means used to gain this victory, no one denied that Glasgow's first Great Exhibition had been a success much larger than even the most sanguine had dared imagine. Closing day left a sense of great emptiness intensified by happy memories of the summer. Meanwhile the Eiffel Tower was going up in Paris.

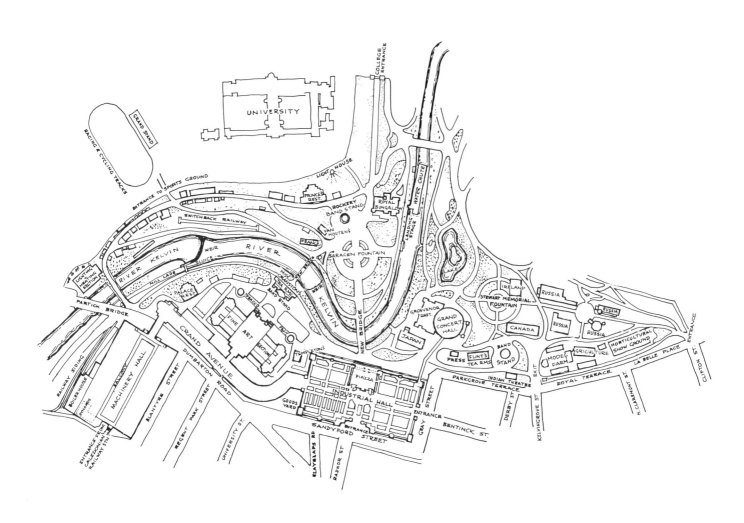

54. The Glasgow International Exhibition, 1901, held in Kelvingrove Park. (Based on the official plan.)

1901

55. The Industrial Hall, the Exhibition's main building, from the north. To the left is what remained of Kelvingrove Mansion after recent demolition work: painted white it served as the Japanese pavilion. Seats in the foreground are arranged around the Rockery Bandstand.

The 1888 Exhibition left an indelible impression on the citizens of Glasgow. After the buildings had been regretfully cleared away, the Association for the Promotion of Art and Music turned its attention to plans for the grand new Art Gallery and Museum, incorporating a School of Art and a hall for music, which was to be 1888's permanent memorial. The Exhibition's clear profits of approximately £43,000 were more than doubled by public subscription, while the Corporation gave part of the Kelvingrove site. A competition in 1892 secured a design fairly universally disdained today, and the foundation stone was laid by the Duke of York in 1897.[1] The idea of a second exhibition to inaugurate the building was proposed in the same year and found sponsors worth £195,000 by October. The guarantee fund closed at £580,916.

The dawn of the new century seemed an appropriate time for an exhibition. Satisfaction with the achievements of the past underpinned an atmosphere of secure optimism about the future. The exhibition would show the progress in Industry, Science and Art of all nations during the nineteenth century; it would be 'a resting place for pioneers' from which they could start with new hopes, new courage, new inspiration. 1901 also marked the jubilee of the Great Crystal Palace Exhibition, a challenge which Glasgow could appropriately take up. The 1890s had seen its emergence as a leading centre of progressive art and design, a development undoubtedly catalysed by the 1888 Exhibition. In painting the 'Glasgow Boys' had won recognition as a School of importance, and in the applied arts the distinctive work of 'Glasgow Style' designers was beginning to make its mark. Clydeside's record in manufacturing and engineering had been acknowledged for rather longer. Claiming with new assurance to be 'the first municipality in the world and the second city of the British Empire',[2] Glasgow was eager to assert its status again.

At the same time the outbreak of the Boer War in 1899 had given British imperial and military confidence an unpleasant knock. There was an unconsciously therapeutic impulse underlying the Exhibition's further aim of providing 'a full illustration of the British Empire', and a heightened sense of the value of asserting peaceful relations with foreign neighbours. The death of Queen Victoria in January of 1901 seemed to confirm the ending of an era, and together with the unexpected prolongation of war in South Africa set a background of lurking insecurity which the Exhibition set itself to transcend.

Paris had in fact made first claim on the twentieth century, with the great Exposition Universelle of 1900. Glasgow was honour-bound to make 1901 the biggest event yet seen in Britain at least, and to make it properly international. The organisers were able to canvas support in Paris and secure many displays second-hand for Glasgow, but the Exhibition inevitably attracted disparaging comparison with its cosmopolitan Gallic predecessor - though this had been by no means the success hoped for. Otherwise the 1901 Exhibition was very like Glasgow's first - indeed many of the same men were involved in its organisation, including H. A. Hedley, the General Manager. Again this was a mixed blessing: against the advantage of experience was the drawback of persistent nostalgic comparison. Just as none of the later London shows ever recaptured the effect on the popular imagination of the Crystal Palace, so Glasgow's second Exhibition, grand though it was, had too little that was new to generate the special excitement and affection of the first. Comparative admissions figures were published daily, and showed greatly increased attendance. But it soon became clear that the marketing of the Exhibition had outrun its provision of facilities; and that the public's taste for entertainment, sharpened in 1888, was now much more demanding.

The centrepiece of the Exhibition was to be Simpson and Allen's new Art Gallery and Museum, which was eventually completed by the Corporation, wildly over budget at a cost of £257,000, and without the new

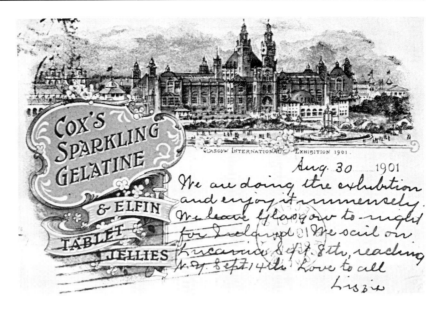

Cox's Sparkling Gelatine & Elfin Tablet Jellies

GLASGOW INTERNATIONAL EXHIBITION 1901.

Aug. 30 1901

We are doing the exhibition and enjoy it immensely. We leave Glasgow to-night for Ireland. We sail on *Lucania* Sept. 8th, reaching N.Y. Sept 14th. Love to all

Lissie

GLASGOW EXHIBITION.
Sandyford Street, looking East.

Dear E, So sorry forgot your birthday. But was at Arran

56 and 57. Picture postcards were a recent invention in 1901: the back was (by law) given over entirely to the address, leaving little room for messages. Top, the Art Gallery and Museum, with Miss Cranston's Tea House in front: the advertising potential of postcards was obvious. Bottom, the Sandyford Street entrance to the Industrial Hall, showing one of the Corporation's newly electrified trams. The originals are coloured.

School of Art (this was separately constructed to designs by Charles Rennie Mackintosh and the eastern section opened in 1899). It was generally felt that Glasgow had done itself proud with what was hailed in the *Official Catalogue* as 'one of the most elaborate edifices devoted to Art in Europe'. Predictably enough there were some who preferred the intimacy of the old museum, the late eighteenth-century Kelvingrove Mansion, and local protest at plans to demolish it to clear space for the Exhibition Concert Hall forced an awkward delay. In the end it went, though to add insult to outrage its 1876 extension was reprieved and became the Japanese pavilion for the Exhibition.

Given the space occupied by the permanent Art Galleries, and the ambitious scale of the enterprise, the site in Kelvingrove Park, though larger than before, presented some planning problems. The Crystal Palace concept of 1888, which attempted to house practically everything under one spectacular roof, was necessarily abandoned for a curious version of

the decentralisation then popular in exhibition layouts. The functions of 1888's Main Building were divided between the new Art Galleries and separate Industrial, Machinery and Concert Halls. The Machinery Hall actually found itself on the other side of a public road, but with proper regard for the climate it was connected to the main site by a covered fly-over and 'Grand Avenue', which ran via the Art Galleries to the Industrial Hall. So the 'serious' part of the Exhibition was still effectively in one giant piece. Minor buildings for Agriculture, and Heating and Lighting, took up some overflow, as did a number of the individual foreign pavilions which had been popular since the Paris Exposition of 1867. Also appearing in 1901 were several separate commercial structures, the forerunners of the great company buildings which together with national pavilions were to dominate twentieth-century exhibitions.

The Art Gallery and Museum ('ornate yet chaste' to admirers, 'far too much a casino . . . sadly wanting in sobriety, and restfulness, and dignity' to critics[3]) dictated not only the layout but the architectural style of the Exhibition. Built in a pinky-brown sandstone, its Jacobean-cum-Spanish Renaissance style was intended to complement Sir Gilbert Scott's Gothic

58. The gleaming temporary Industrial Hall adjacent to the permanent new Art Gallery and Museum, which was opened at the Exhibition. In the centre is the Saracen Fountain, presented to the City by Walter Macfarlane and Co. The strange lump protruding above Miss Cranston's Tea House is the back of the Shell Bandstand. Van Houten's Cocoa Kiosk is on the far right.

University across the river. Adding another link to the chain of conservatism, the Exhibition's Executive opted for designs submitted by James
Miller, in a style he connected with that of the sixteenth-century Spanish
Renaissance. The effect of his Industrial Hall, the Exhibition's chief
building, was generally perceived as 'Oriental' when it was built, and
enthusiastically praised as impressive and thoroughly appropriate. Poster-
ity, seeing things from a different perspective, is disappointed that
Glasgow's leading avant-garde architect was not given his head, especially
in view of the rampant Art Nouveau of Paris the year before and Turin the
year after. But designs by Charles Rennie Mackintosh were not surprisingly rejected. Despite the commission for the School of Art, which came
through the enlightenment of Fra Newbery, and a growing reputation on
the continent, Mackintosh's work was generally regarded in his home city
as uncomfortably odd. The 'Glasgow Style' as a whole hardly had the
airing it deserved at the Exhibition. However some of the restaurants and
pavilions, designed by various hands, did strike a more contemporary
note, with their clean lines, projecting eaves and stencilled decoration.
Indeed the reactionary found in them 'a little too much of L'Art

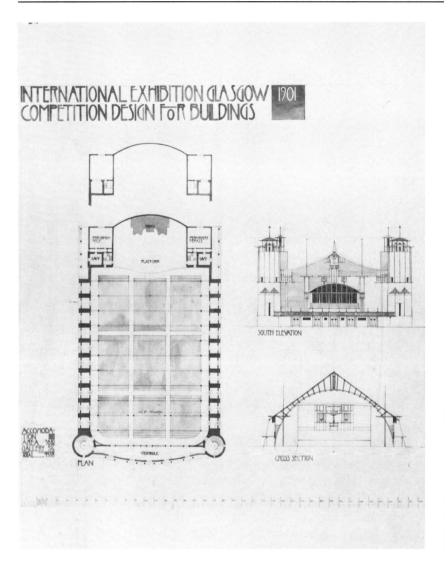

INTERNATIONAL EXHIBITION GLASGOW 1901
COMPETITION DESIGN FOR BUILDINGS

SOUTH ELEVATION

PLAN

CROSS SECTION

59. The Concert Hall which was not built: a design from a set submitted unsuccessfully by Glasgow's most famous architect, Charles Rennie Mackintosh, working in the firm of Honeyman and Keppie where he became a partner in 1901.

60 (*opposite*). George Walton, another leading exponent of the 'Glasgow Style', designed this studio above the rockery for T. & R. Annan, the Exhibition's official photographers.

Nouveau'. The prevailing whiteness of the buildings reflected the strong influence on exhibition architecture of Chicago's 1893 'White City'. The monumental Beaux Arts style which went with it was too close to Glasgow's own classicizing tradition to have been taken up: 'something different' was the prime requirement of exhibition architecture.

Like Sellars' design for 1888, Miller's 'Eastern Palace' offered the fantasy and extravagance craved by the general public at a reasonable cost, this time through the effective use of prefabricated panels of plaster on a sacking base, formed in moulds. Half a million yards of cloth were said to have been used. The plain work was done in boards of the material nailed to a wooden frame and stuccoed over. The frothing white and gold which replaced 1888's strong colours emphasised the permanence, even as it temporarily eclipsed the glory, of the adjacent Art Galleries. Roofs were red, and cupolas felted and painted green to resemble copper. The Grand Dome which again provided the building's focal point was originally golden, though the weather reduced it to a silvery gleam. Miller had

61. The Grand Central Dome, gilded and topped with the figure of Light, seen from the grounds. The piazza between its façade and the colonnade was a popular social spot, 'a veritable Mitchell Library of human nature' on warm evenings.

lavished his special attention on the elaboration of this central section, which was accounted by some 'a perfect masterpiece of design, marked by a grace and dignity that make the neighbouring Art Galleries ... seem trumpery by comparison'.[4] Hopes were expressed (as they had been in the case of 1888's dome) that it might be preserved after the Exhibition for public use. At 180 ft it was higher than its predecessor, and topped by a golden angel - 'Light' personified - bearing an electric torch.

The Dome's décor within was not highly rated. It featured two more gigantic angels in 'art' shades of green, pale red, and violet, floating in the hemisphere above the obligatory allegorical figures - four pairs representing 'Industry', 'Art', 'Science' and 'Commerce' (more appropriate to Glasgow than 1888's 'Agriculture') - set in a conventional landscape. Sculpted figures on ship's prows dominated the corners. The ensemble was completed by four scriptural texts (different from 1888's) and the names of eighteen great men, including Watt and Kelvin along with Phidias, Shakespeare and Beethoven. Two electric elevators to the Dome balconies, once they were working, took visitors up for a fine view over the city.

Presiding over the Dome, the Exhibition's main meeting place, was an outsize statue of King Edward VII (so large indeed that it was claimed to

BENEATH THE DOME.

62. Beneath the Dome: a view evoking the grand extent of the interior. While Albert Hodge's sculpted figures depicting 'The Triumph of Navigation' were admired, his 18 ft statue of the new king, Edward VII, came in for much ridicule.

be 'prolific of misunderstandings': one was advised to specify 'under King Edward's nose' to be sure of a rendez-vous). This had been hastily knocked up in addition to the other figure work by Albert Hodge (a sculptor working in London but trained at the Glasgow School of Art) after the death in January of Queen Victoria. It was the first statue to be raised in His Majesty's honour, but was not altogether a success: the monarch's 'stiff and conscious pose appears to be the result of a somewhat undignified effort to balance the small crown on his head'. However the new King (who had been booked to open the Exhibition as the Prince of Wales) did not make himself available in person. Nor did his heir, the Duke of Cornwall. The event which styled itself the largest and most important exhibition ever staged in Britain was opened by the Princess Louise, Duchess of Fife.

Dearly as the Duchess was loved, this was a severe blow to civic pride. Furthermore the opening ceremony was cast at the King's request into half-mourning, to the undoubted fury of many Corporation wives. However 2 May 1901 dawned brilliantly and good humour prevailed as the Duchess unlocked the Grand Entrance with a golden key, before moving on to exercise a second key on the new Art Galleries. Altogether an atmosphere 'of unclouded brightness that is rare in our sombre city' was

thought certain to have made a favourable impression on the Duchess, on what was her first visit to Glasgow, and it was earnestly hoped that the monarch would come to the Exhibition later in the year, after hearing from his daughter of its glories. He did not, and Glasgow had to content itself with the monstrous statue. However the unnaturally good weather persisted - April and May were the best in living memory - and visitors poured eagerly into the Exhibition.

Pride of place went to the Fine Art Section in the splendid new Galleries, advertised as 'the greatest art Collection ever gathered under one roof'. It was indisputably an improvement on 1888's somewhat indiscriminate display, being restricted to paintings, sculpture and objets d'art on loan, offering a major survey of nineteenth-century art. English painting was shown 'with remarkable completeness': among those with the most works to their names were Turner, David Cox, Sam Bough and Millais. The Pre-Raphaelites in general were well represented: one of the finest, Burne-Jones' *Danaë* or *The Tower of Brass*, was presented to the city in June by William Connal, a local pig-iron manufacturer. The foreign contribution was less full, though gaps in the French and Dutch sections were judged 'surprisingly few'.[5] But while there were many

63. The royal party arriving outside the Industrial Hall on opening day. The mosque-like structure on the right is the pavilion of James Templeton and Co., the famous Glasgow carpet manufacturer.

paintings by Corot and the Marises, there were very few French Impressionists. Despite some local feeling that Scottish artists should have been more prominent, native painting was in fact well represented. The work of the Glasgow Boys, most of whom were now comfortably established (Lavery and Henry were on the sub-committee) was modestly but evenly shown.

64. *La princesse du pays de la porcelaine*, by J. A. McNeill Whistler, one of many treasures lent to the Exhibition by William Burrell. It is now in Whistler's Peacock Room in the Freer Gallery of Art, Washington, DC.

65 (*right*). The Kodak was seen everywhere at this Exhibition; photography had become popular with ladies since Queen Alexandra had taken it up. The 'humour' of this vignette is characteristic of the period. Foreign visitors, even the French, were generally surprised and impressed by the size of the Exhibition.

The sculpture section, again organised by Fra Newbery, was similar in scope to 1888's, but the conditions in which it was displayed, among potted palms in the spacious central hall, were in pleasing contrast. British sculpture was well supported by foreign contributions. Among works subsequently acquired for the city were Rodin's plasters of *John the Baptist* and *A Burger of Calais* (£60 each). Newbery was also convener of the Architecture Section: it included one or two examples of 'the latest ideas' which were viewed as original but eccentric. The Arts and Crafts and Schools of Art sections in two of the Gallery's corner pavilions did not attract much attention, but here the fruits of Newbery's vitalising changes at the Glasgow School of Art, and his establishment of the Technical Art Studios in 1892, were clearly visible. A generation of students had been encouraged to develop a wide range of craft skills and a distinctive style in design. While Fine Art remained an almost exclusively male preserve, Decorative Art must have seemed close to take-over by women. Exhibiting here were Jessie King, Ann Macbeth, Marion and Margaret Wilson, Phoebe Traquair and others too numerous to mention. The Photography Section made an international impression, through the connections established by its convener, J. Craig Annan, with leading photo-

E

graphers like the American Alfred Stieglitz. Also comfortably absorbed into the new Galleries were the important Scottish archaeological and historical relics which had crowded the Bishop's Palace in 1888. There were 3036 of them this time, again organised by Dr David Murray. Trophies from the battlefields of South Africa struck a more topical note.

The furnishing of the Royal Reception Rooms by the North Entrance of the Industrial Hall - a hallway, Louis XV style drawing room and 'Jacobethan' dining room - offered space for some choice pre-nineteenth-century paintings and antiques. Politic recognition was offered to the Glasgow ship-owner who was to become the municipality's greatest artistic benefactor by asking Mr William Burrell to arrange the dining room. He was also on the Art Objects committee. Overall he lent more than 200 pieces to the Exhibition - paintings and much more - a foretaste of the astonishing riches of the collection he was to give to the city in 1944.

Exhibits in the great 700 x 360 ft Industrial Hall were categorised more broadly than in 1888 into eight classes. There was also less control over the appearance of the interior. Miller had met the Executive's demand for an unencumbered space with structural panache; but the shortage of

COME AWA'
TAMMAS!"
'WAIT A WEE,
KIRSTY,THERE'S
SOMETHING
IN MA
E'E."

columns to contribute a sense of vista and spatial order exacerbated the general effect of confusion. Great advances in taste and techniques of display were claimed for the last decade. Substantial investment in presentation was evident, with many stands designed as individual pavilions. There was some 'breaking away from the gingerbread show-case style of design which has hitherto been considered elegant and appropriate, ... a happy augury of the closer relation which may be expected to exist between Art and Commerce in the new century'.[6] But again the opportunity to exploit progressive design talents of the highest order was almost wholly ignored in favour of the safely conventional, and the overall effect was disappointing. There were however one or two bright spots of innovation which attracted critical attention.

Mackintosh himself had been commissioned to design four stands[7] but otherwise seems to have turned his back on the Exhibition. He and his wife Margaret Macdonald, Frances (her sister) and Herbert Macnair, 'The Four', looked instead to the Turin Exhibition of 1902 where they exhibited for Scotland to critical acclaim. George Walton however (brother of Glasgow Boy E. A. Walton), another designer-decorator from the GSA, did take space, and his room-sets won approving notice. But the most ambitious exercise in the 'modern spirit' was the pavilion of the local furnishing firm Wylie and Lochhead, which stood out brilliantly from its competitors. Behind a striking exterior designed by David Gow three designers who worked for the firm were given control over every detail of separate rooms - John Ednie the dining room, E. A. Taylor the drawing room, and George Logan the 'Rossetti Library' and a lady's bedroom. All

66 and 67 (*opposite*). A fine collection of sculpture was elegantly displayed in the central hall of the new Kelvingrove Art Gallery and Museum: a marked improvement on 1888's cramped gallery. In the foreground is *Hypnos bestowing sleep* by Fehr. 'Art' of this sort was an eye-opener to many Scots.

68. The drawing room designed in 'advanced artistic' style by E. A. Taylor, in the pavilion of the furnishing firm Wylie and Lochhead. The walls were in willow-green silk with white enamelled woodwork, and some of the furniture was stained purple. Other details harmonised in tints of green and violet.

69. The exterior of Wylie and Lochhead's pavilion on the Main Avenue of the Industrial Hall. Design at the Exhibition was in general rather conventional and this display, representing a commercial form of the 'Glasgow Style', was widely approved by progressive critics.

the designers were connected with the GSA, or with the often overlooked Glasgow and West of Scotland Technical College, as students and teachers. Newbery's policy of forging strong personal and practical links with local industries was here amply justified. Simple lines, lovingly used organic motifs (roses, bluebells, butterflies, birds) and co-ordinating colours (the soft rose, purple, green and grey beloved of the Glasgow Style) unified the interior without spoiling the effect of individuality. For the modestly affluent middle-class market they wished to attract, Wylie and Lochhead could now offer an elegant modern style, a more homely, less frightening version of the experimental designs produced by Mackintosh and his associates in the 1890s. (The firm could of course reassure conservative customers with the revivalist styles in which it had carried out the decoration of the Royal Reception Rooms.) The pavilion was widely reviewed and selected entire for the British Arts and Crafts Exhibition in Budapest the following year. And it brought hard commissions, ranging from the furnishing and decoration throughout of Mrs Coats' new home in Handsworth, Birmingham for about £300, to the more lavish requirements of William Weir, the engineering magnate. So while the Exhibition did not make any major new artistic statement, it was nevertheless important in transmitting the Glasgow Style to a wider public.

Heal's from London was showing the pretty oak bedroom, designed by Ambrose Heal, Jun., which had won two gold medals at Paris. It allowed an interesting comparison between the more folksy flavour of the English Arts and Crafts style and the distinctively urban chic of Glasgow's. W. A. S. Benson was another prominent designer attracted from the South. He erected a pavilion in the grounds to display his firm's speciality in art metalwork and light fittings, together with the artistic wallpapers of Jeffrey and Co. of Islington. Also now specialising in light fittings, though

70. Reaction from the hard to impress.

GLASGOW MAN— "WHAT DO YOU THINK O' THE EXHIBITION?"
DUNDEE MAN— "IT'S NO BAD FOR GLASGOW!"

71. Advertisement in the Exhibition catalogue for the growing department store, Pettigrew and Stephens. The firm was interested in contemporary style, as is shown by the graphics here, and commissioned Mackintosh to design its stand in the Women's Section.

72. Scots came home for the Exhibition from all parts.

more conventional in design, was the glass firm Osler's. Their popular 'electric fountain' near the Dome was a pleasant reminder of the famous Crystal Fountain they had made fifty years earlier for the Great Exhibition.

Food manufacturers in particular now understood the importance of attractive presentation. Fry and Sons for example set off their chocolates with mauve and gilt; Glendinning's Beef and Malt Wine won notice for its miniature pavilion, as did the 'striking originality and new colourings' of Lipton's stand. Heinz of Pittsburg displayed its wares, including baked beans, very handsomely and handed out both samples and a novel 'charm' to visitors. The sales potential of samples, especially in tempting a conservative public to new foods, like the Protene Company's mysterious 'nourishing and sustaining substance', was widely recognised. Free cigarettes distributed from Stephen Mitchell's elegant cream and gold stall, manned with 'Oriental' operatives, doubtless gave them the edge over their Glasgow rivals F. and J. Smith, whose much larger display included two machines - though the mandatory Turkish-clad hand-rollers were added for picturesqueness.

Rivalry between Glasgow's department stores was carried into the Exhibition as this form of shopping grew in popularity. Forsyth's, specialising in male clothing, chose the industrial approach, with its latest loom, operated by female attendants, turning out its 'Hygienic' woollen underwear six at a time. Aiming more shrewdly at the feminine market (they also exhibited in the Women's Section), Pettigrew and Stephens went for glamour, with a charming Moorish pavilion housing a display of

73 and 74. Pretty female attendants were used wherever possible. (Four of the 'Turkish' cigarette girls allegedly came from Manchester and four from Birmingham). (*Bailie*)

silks and two Irish girls at hand looms. Pretty girls were exploited throughout the Exhibition - Quaker Oats Quakeresses, Swiss chocolate maids and the like. The welfare of the 500 or so female attendants, many of them far from home, became an object of philanthropic concern to members of the Ladies' Committee: a Girl's Club was opened to provide pianos, easy chairs and a comfortable shoulder to cry on within the Exhibition.

Gimmicks repeated some of the formulae of 1888. Coats of Paisley, which had by now absorbed its rival Clark's (an early amalgamation which secured later survival) chose the Eddystone lighthouse for recreation, on a

75. (*left*) Pettigrew and Stephens' main stand was a 'Moorish' structure, facing the conservative frontage of their rivals Forsyth's. At the entrance to the Grand Avenue connecting the Industrial Hall with the Machinery Hall is the genuine Moroccan pavilion, built by a party of Moors.

scale of 1:20, in sewing thread spools of appropriate shades. Isdale and McCallum did statuettes in soap of the King and Queen - and Robert Burns and Walter Scott too for good measure. But a pair of large marzipan polar bears from John Buchanan and Bros was a new inspiration. The Oxford University Press attracted attention by suspending its English Dictionary on a 3-inch strip of the fine strong India paper which had revolutionised the Bible trade.

Among the attractive displays of consumer goods, the machine guns and (dummy) explosives of Nobel's large stand on the Main Avenue came as something of a shock: people tended to hurry past when they realised what they were looking at. Automobiles were a genuine novelty, examined with fascination. Two Glasgow manufacturers (Robert Mitchell and Stirling's Motor Carriages Ltd) were exhibiting motor-cars in the Hall, alongside the carriages which they would displace. General trials of reliability were also held, in keeping with exhibition commitment to the competitive testing of goods, and the machines attracted crowds in the grounds after their daily runs.

Women's contribution, it was acknowledged, would necessarily be a significant feature in this twentieth-century exhibition, and so it was. The

76. Exhibition automobile trials were based on the new sports arena which had been constructed on the University athletics ground.

Women's Committee was supported again by a formidable array of titles, and led by a professional, Miss Tessa Mackenzie, who had previously run sections of London shows. The 450-odd places on the Exhibition's other active committees were filled exclusively by men. Occupying the east corner, fenced in by foreigners, the section was separate but substantial. Arrangement was more methodical than in 1888, adopting five classes: Trades; Education; Applied Art and Handicraft; Nursing and Philanthropy; and Science, Literature and Music. The aim was to give a 'comprehensive representation of the variety of . . . work in which women can now take part', though again the perspective was thoroughly middle-class and disguised the true economic importance of working-class women. Nevertheless compared with Paris, where the Palais de Femme had been devoted almost exclusively to fashion (though contributions from women appeared in some other sections), it was a serious show. Miss Mackenzie had gathered many exhibits in Paris, making this, as in 1888, a genuinely international display. The French themselves were represented only in the Education section because of what was indicated to be a foolish over-reaction to a smallpox scare.

In the 'Trades' section a Miss Hood exhibited photography as remunerative employment. More significantly women from the flourishing Scottish Co-operative Wholesale Society were shown at sewing machines supplying an expanding market in ready-made clothing. This was an extension of the traditional female connection with spinning and weaving, and like the displays of homespun tweeds focussed on the individual skilled operative. Pettigrew and Stephens, well aware that their fortunes rested with the middle-class money-spending woman, took pains with their exhibit in this section, commissioning a stall from Mackintosh to house a display of quality lace, with two Belgian lace-makers at work and a saleswoman to drive home the advantage. 'Applied Art and Handicraft' was the richest and most international division. The great growth of women's work in this area in the last decade was particularly noticeable in Glasgow, where a number of the small craft studios which proliferated in the 1890s were set up by women (like the Gilmour, Wilson and Macdonald sisters). Many female designers were exhibiting, as mentioned above, in the crafts section of Fine Art. From visitors to the Women's Section there were again some complaints that local work was insufficiently prominent. The Glasgow School of Art was responsible here for the display of book-binding, enclosed in an austerely latticed stall which Mackintosh had designed in striking contrast to the bulbous lines of his stand for Pettigrew and Stephens. Other working exhibits included wood-carving and metal-working. Enamels were eye-catching and needlework as before well represented, including a decorative panel by Mrs Walter Crane to her husband's design.

'Education' was dominated by the Schools of Cookery, and Housewifery and Domestic Science which had been springing up in response to a preoccupation with hygiene at the end of the nineteenth century. It was also felt that 'the servantless age, to which we are being forced to look

77. Caricature of one thought likely to approve the high ideals of the Women's Section. In fact it was generally popular. (*Bailie*)

78. The latticing used in Mackintosh's new Glasgow School of Art building is echoed in the stand he designed for the School's contribution to the Women's Section - 'a sort of cage in which to confine a pair of lady bookbinders', in green and white wood, panelled with linen.

forward' would hold fewer terrors for one properly trained in the lighting of fires, etc. Less basic concerns were also evident: the Glasgow School of Cookery won special approval for its realistic marzipan carrots and potatoes, a 'much more desirable accomplishment to the average young lady than the prosaic ability to bone a turkey'. A newer development was the 'practical and scientific training of gentlewomen' in horticulture and the lighter branches of agriculture offered by institutions like the Lady Warwick Hostel, Reading. 'Literature and Music' (Science did not materialise) made 'an interesting corner', while 'Philanthropy', an important outlet for many energetic women of the upper classes, was well represented. Fine white seams and embroidery by the deaf, dumb, blind, poor and criminal were the visible results. The various organisations exhibiting included the Royal Repository for the Sale of Gentlewomen's Work, a valuable service for the impoverished class-bound genteel, and the British Temperance Women's Association.

Connecting the Industrial Hall with the Machinery Section was the Grand Avenue, an impressive covered walkway 1000 ft long and 75 ft wide, with high glazed semi-circular roof. It offered prime display space, and running down the centre for much of its length was a fine show of the ship models which had been so striking in 1888. They were chronologically arranged to exemplify the development of shipping during the nineteenth century. Other models were on show in the Machinery Hall. At the turn of the century something approaching one in two of the ships plying the world were Clyde built or powered - an astonishing and poignant statistic. Pride of place went to the newest and biggest vessels - like Fairfield's HMS *Good Hope*, the largest and fastest armoured cruiser afloat, and the great warship *Asahi* built in 1899 for Japan. Visitors marvelling at these flagships of Glasgow's prosperity overlooked their warning of Clydeside's vulnerability in its increasing reliance on massive naval orders from home and abroad.

Displays in the rest of the Grand Avenue manifested the peculiar and wonderful variety of the universal exhibition. They included machinery for wood-carving and for dredging; sewing machines from Singer's, an important Glasgow employer, and carpet sweepers from another Amer-

MODEL BOATS
IN THE
GRAND AVENUE-
CRITICAL ATTITUDE

ican firm, Bissell's. The Burmah Oil Co. had erected a teakwood Burmese pagoda. At the 'Dido' umbrella stand you could choose a stick and watch your umbrella being made; then move on to examine a Palestine encampment for Thomas Cook's tourists in the Holy Land. A loom displayed a new dress fabric, 'Wincella', invented by John McArthur of Ayr, while at a 'pretty little stand' on the covered bridge, R. G. Scotland, the truss and artificial limb maker, had his wares 'neatly arranged'.

The Grand Avenue delivered visitors at the gallery level of the mighty Machinery Hall. The incorporation into the Exhibition of the six and a half acre Bunhouse site (now occupied by Kelvin Hall) allowed an increase of almost a third in the space available, which had been under severe

79 (*opposite*). Locomotives took a prominent place in the great Machinery Hall. The 'oriental' conservatory in the centre was put up by Walter Macfarlane and Co. to display the firm's ornamental ironwork.

80 (*opposite below*). As in 1888 model vessels were a top attraction. (*Bailie*)

81 (*right*). Advertisement from the catalogue: Dubs, a German, had left partnership with Walter Neilson to set up a rival works in 1864. The firm was the second largest of the three Glasgow locomotive builders, themselves the biggest in Britain, which amalgamated in 1903.

STAND Nos. 364, 524.

DŬBS & C⁰·

Glasgow Locomotive Works,

GLASGOW,

MANUFACTURERS OF

DŬBS' PATENT CRANE-LOCOMOTIVE

LOCOMOTIVE

"ABT" MOUNTAIN CLIMBER.

ENGINES.

N. G. R.

LONDON ADDRESS: 16 VICTORIA STREET, WESTMINSTER.

pressure in 1888. It also exploited existing railway sidings, and separated noisy machinery from the more consumer-oriented parts of the Exhibition. James Miller's original employment in Glasgow as an architect with the Caledonian Railway Company prepared him admirably for the design of this great steel structure, 500 x 320 ft, with a central span of 108 ft 6 in.

Gazing down upon the vast 'Hall of Vulcan', many a visitor might have shared the thoughts of the *Official Guide*, contemplating 'a significance and a power for changing the conditions of labour such as machines never before possessed'. Here were shown the triumphs of the nineteenth century and hints of those to come. Visitors who thrilled to this noise and power had no inkling of the devastation that the twentieth century had in store. Important competitors were in evidence, and there was a sense of gathering pace - 'nowadays an expensive machine may be thrown out after a few months' use' - but as yet no fear that Glasgow could not compete. Most of the local exhibitors were naturally the same as in 1888, many of them family businesses. Their skill in the manufacture of specialist parts was Glasgow's pride but also its ruin in a new era of mass-production. But in 1901 the well-known names inspired self-satisfaction and exultation in the existing achievements of the Workshop of the World.

The locomotives which had been squeezed out in 1888 took their rightful place. Four companies were exhibiting: Andrew Barclay of Kilmarnock; Dubs; Sharp, Stewart and Co.; and Neilson, Reid and Co., the largest locomotive works in Britain. (The amalgamation of the last three in 1903 made North British Locomotives the largest works outside America. This great industry has now disappeared from Glasgow.) Together with steamship models exhibited in the Machinery Section by firms like Beardmore (formerly R. Napier's), the locos offered a palpable and stirring representation of the lines of communication which held the civilised world together. Lord Kelvin's new telephone exchange displayed the beginnings of a mysterious invisible network.

82. One of the most popular working displays. (*Bailie*)

Processes with domestic application were the easiest to display to the general public. The Glasgow Herald exhibited an electrically driven newspaper printing machine; while a working laundry, with washing machines, hydro-extractor and ironing machine, dealt with 100 sheets in approximately 45 minutes. The Bermaline Bakery of Partick manufactured its famous bread on the spot, and supplied the Scottish passion for buns and cakes in its sale room. The firm clinched its appeal with the great sugar model of the Industrial Hall, 4 ft 6 in x 9 ft and illuminated inside, 'one of the most ambitious things ever attempted in sugar'. Stewart and Young's showed a sugar reproduction of the birthplace of Robert Burns, 'the sweetest singer for all time', as part of their confectionery display, which was counted one of the principal sights of the Exhibition. The sweet Scottish tooth has indeed meant big business ever since sugar became one of Glasgow's staple imports in the eighteenth century. At the end of the nineteenth century Scottish manufacturers were turning out more than 1000 tons of sweet stuff a week, much of it for export, and

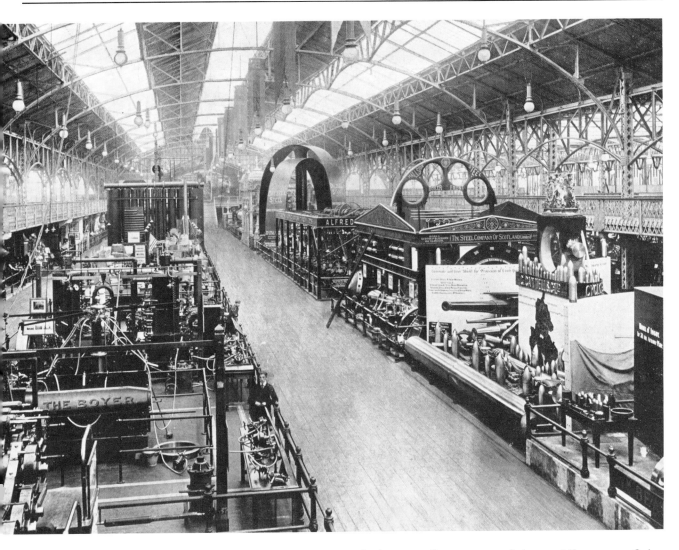

83. A fine view of the Machinery Hall, showing the dominating steel arches of Colville's Dalzell Steelworks and the Steel Company of Scotland's stand. In the foreground right are the gleaming guns and shells of C. Cammell and Co. and the end of William Beardmore's display of armour-plating. A Boyer engine heads the row of basic machinery exhibits to the left.

Glasgow was producing over 80 per cent of the world's sugar-refining equipment. On show at the Exhibition were the latest technical innovations in confectionery machinery using the vacuum principle and a steam coil system. But ominously perhaps the new plant exhibited by the Glasgow firm of Assafrey was made in Dresden.

Many manufacturers of less appealing products made the extra effort with their displays which attracted general notice. Colville's, by 1900 the largest Scottish steel producer, erected a huge double arch of bent steel plates, while Weir's drew attention to their range of pumps with a 40 ft wide waterfall 'enhanced by myriads of electric lights and artistic oriental painted woodwork'. The majority of firms however concentrated on no-nonsense demonstrations to potential buyers. W. G. Riddell records the wretchedness of countless evenings spent as a young engineer with his boss, who had bought him a season ticket, hanging over all the latest machines.[8] Major external competitors were attracted to this important market, among them the Manchester firm Mather and Platt with probably the biggest heavy machinery stand in the Hall, including a complete

GLASGOW INTERNATIONAL EXHIBITION.
MESS⁣ʳˢ G.&J. WEIR'S PUMPS & WATERFALL,
MACHINERY HALL.

84. An 'art nouveau' postcard produced by G. and J. Weir showing the waterfall erected by the firm at the end of the Machinery Hall to demonstrate its pumps.

bleaching plant, a little electric conveyor, and many working models. A significant display of American machinery utilising compressed air, comparatively novel in Scotland but exploited by 'our cousins' for some time, was shown by the Ingersoll Sergeant Drill Company of London. A firm of American origin which, following Singer's example had established a factory locally, at Renfrew in 1897, was Babcock and Wilcox.

Non-Glasgow firms were prominent among those prepared to pay for the extra exposure offered by a separate building. Among those sited in the North Gardens were the Bullard Machine Tool Co. and Churchill's showing a further range of machinery from the USA, and international firms from London like Selig Sonnenthal, and Schuckert's. The Patent Paraffin Gas Lighting Co. and two acetylene gas manufacturers built individual pavilions to persuade the public of the merits and safety of their new fuels. The Heating and Lighting Building however seems to have lost visitors who would certainly have been interested in its collection of the latest gas and oil domestic appliances through its functional appearance and misleading title.

While dynamos and electric motors had lost some of their glamour in the years since 1888, the Exhibition was an important showcase for the energy of the twentieth century. It was estimated that four fifths of the power developed in the great boiler house was converted into electricity. But perhaps most notable was its application outside the Exhibition, in the newly electrified tram system which carried thousands to and from the gates that summer. The Tramways had been taken over by the Corporation in 1894, and after the first electrified section opened in 1898, the enormous task of modernising the whole service in time for the opening of the Exhibition was undertaken by the dynamic new manager, John Young – a good example of the tendency of exhibitions to galvanise local improvements. The lighting contracts for the Exhibition buildings again followed the principle of a fair showing for different systems. In the illumination of the grounds a straight fight between electricity in the East Gardens and high pressure gas in the North and West, the biggest installation of its kind, led to widespread complaints of too much candle power. 'It spoils

85. The Industrial Hall piazza illuminated on a rainy night.

the effect of the buildings, its dazzling brightness is uncomfortable, and - worst of all - it is utterly unbecoming to the complexion.' Twilight enchantment was preferred.

It was in relation to the machinery exhibits that the educational purpose of the Exhibition was most clearly expressed - and forthrightly linked to commercial benefit. The Executive was anxious to point out that there was a representative display of machines and tools from Glasgow's key competitors Germany and the USA, though neither was officially represented. 'The British workman is no dullard ...; who knows that our own Clyde workmen may improve on the machines they will see here - and thereby bring credit and increased prosperity to our grand old city. The educational value of the Exhibition cannot be overestimated, and if it only has the effect of stimulating the energies of our workmen, the Executive will feel that their labours have not been in vain.'[9] There was approving comment on the 'simply amazing' number of season tickets sold to young working men and women who were 'not all frivolous', and whose 'look of real earnestness' as they entered showed their awareness of the practical utility of the Exhibition.[10] Complaints that the hours of opening of the Machinery Section (10.00-1.00, 2.00-5.00, 6.00-7.30) were inconsistent with the aim of educating the working man brought a swift change to 11.00–9.00.

A significant international contribution was clearly important for the Exhibition's educational purpose, but even more for its general prestige. Here the Executive could claim a major advance on 1888, which was acknowledged in retrospect to have 'scarcely merited the dignity of the term "international". Today it is different!' The foreign press, which had been 'not a little ignorant' of Glasgow's size and commercial activity, was said to be 'flabbergasted' at the magnitude of the Exhibition.[11] Some comment was more scathing: 'every section of the Paris exhibition offered more to the public than the whole industrial hall at Glasgow ... International Exhibition? What a delusion! ... Can a fair of this nature be taken seriously ... ? There is nothing but a provincial exhibition of local, or perhaps national, Scotch interest, but foreign countries have sent nothing but market-ware, stock things from Paris ...'[12] Such scorn was rare. And whatever the press might say, for the thousands of visitors who had never been to England, let alone Paris, the foreign displays were new and fascinating.

With war continuing in South Africa, the display of Empire, one of the Exhibition's stated purposes, acquired a special patriotic edge. The exhibits quite accurately reflected the relationship of the different members to the 'mother' country whose prosperity they fed. The Dominion of Canada exhibited its civilised and established status with a display of furniture, fabrics, organs and pianos alongside cold storage plant in the Industrial Hall. It emphasised its autonomy with a handsome white pavilion, the second largest, in the grounds, where the centrepiece of the largely agricultural display was the Ottawa Library dome rendered in harvest products. Canada's vigorous new Liberal government was making another push to populate the empty spaces of the West. Australia, absent in 1888, now appeared in force. Although the Australian colonies had become a federal Commonwealth on the first day of 1901 they continued

86. Captured Boer guns displayed outside the Industrial Hall were a reminder of the continuing war in South Africa. In this context the Exhibition's emphasis on the countries of the British Empire was understandable.

87. The large and elegant Canadian Pavilion in the grounds.

88. Queensland's stunning display of mineral resources included a quick-silver fountain (using three tons of mercury illuminated by coloured electric light), and a golden obelisk. (*Glasgow Weekly Herald*)

89. The Indian 'bazaar' in the Industrial Hall promoted craftwork for the western market.

their separate, competitive existence in the Industrial Hall. Queensland stood out with its fabulous display of minerals - pyramids of copper and tin, a gilded obelisk representing thirty years' production (allegedly 550 tons) of gold, and one of the Exhibition's popular attractions, the quick-silver fountain. Wool, preserved meats and a pearl-shell trophy suggested other riches. Advice was on hand in a comfortable reception room for the intending emigrant whose eye had been caught. Western Australia endeavoured to indicate its recent industrial and social progress, but added

F

plenty of gold and quartz and another widely visible pearl-shell trophy. Its effective exhibit of timber prompted the suggestion that the Australian redwoods, notably Jarrah, might oust the current fashion for oak.

Rhodesia was displayed as one of the latest additions to the Empire (1888) and made 'a pretty showing'. Its indigenous people were treated under the heading of natural history. A trophy of native weapons, evidently in recent use, was taken to emphasise the 'newness' of the country, and expressed quite nakedly the relationship of Britain to the conquered peoples of Empire. Ceylon and India were not advertising for white settlers, and their economic importance lay partly in the markets they afforded for British manufactures. Their displays, less prominent than in 1888, comprised the 'luxury' goods produced for western consumers. At Ceylon's 'bungalow', native attendants offered free samples of tea, coffee and cocoa, while the rest of the exhibit was handled by a British importer. India's 'bazaar' was likewise arranged by two firms of Indian exporters. The curiosity value of her humans was directly exploited in the Indian Theatre in the grounds, with its 'varied programmes illustrative of Indian life, Snake Charming, Juggling, etc.', while the Prince's restaurant used Cingalese waiters ('very curious looking fellows they are. But they are very smart and civil at their work, can talk and understand English perfectly, and can tot up your account as cleverly as an auctioneer's clerk.')

90. The performers of the brightly coloured, stencil-decorated Indian Theatre provided some of the side-show entertainment craved by the public. The building, known as 'The Monkey House', was later re-erected at Belvidere Hospital, in tribute to the staff's dedication during the recent outbreak of bubonic plague.

91. While boy smokers were too common to attract much attention, the 'cool cheek' with which this one lit a cigarette for a Theatre Hindoo 'inspired general admiration among the crowd that stood by'. (News)

Exoticism with the added attraction of novelty was offered by some of the 'genuine' foreign contributors on this occasion. The ten Moors who arrived and, smoking continuously, built the romantic Moroccan pavilion at the entrance to the Grand Avenue were a source of great fascination. Persia was also exhibiting: its carved walnut stand was loaded with merchandise of wonderful richness by the importing firm of Akbar, Hadji Ali of London and Manchester. The blatant consumer orientation of many of the foreign displays - Denmark for instance showed only porcelain, pottery and antiques - did not bother the visitors to the Exhibition, but led to a trial of strength with the authorities. Some foreign sections were doing a smart trade in fancy goods in contravention of Exhibition rules - Austria, displaying 'principally nick-nacks' and some new curling pins, was apparently the worst for 'canvassing'. This was a delicate matter as the Executive did not wish to offend the valued foreigners, but a principle was at stake and a court case was brought in June. Commercial gain could not be openly accepted as the reason for exhibiting.

Foreign pavilions in the grounds were a major enhancement of the Exhibition's general atmosphere. Japan had transformed the remains of the old Kelvingrove Mansion with a coat of white paint, a large black sun stuck over the statue of Britannia - 'a touch of artistry' - and a Japanese garden around. Within were displayed the exquisite porcelain, fabrics and

92. Foreign exhibitors were notorious for contravening, or circumventing, the rules against sale of exhibits. (*Bailie*)

93. Irish cottages by the Stewart Fountain.

'chaste artistic knick-knacks' which had a strong attraction for many contemporary artists and designers. Quite different in style was the pair of prettily thatched Irish cottages, with stained glass windows and shamrocks throughout, where weavers at work promoted Ireland's best known industry.

Endemic national rivalry with France was particularly intense in the business of exhibitions, and relations were currently under extra strain because of the Boer War. The main French display in the Industrial Hall concentrated on the food, art and consumer luxuries which supported the claim that France was the cradle of civilisation. Their entry in the *Official Catalogue* was absurdly long, with *curricula vitae*, in French, of all the presidents, vice-presidents and secretaries of the different sections. The Executive was clearly torn between the desire to parade France's participation and the urge to put her in her place, which found an outlet in various

sniping comments: French bands were too expensive, the side-shows at Paris were vulgar, and so on. The French pavilion in the grounds was a disappointingly 'plain, unpretentious place with a roof of corrugated iron'.

The Russian section was the the largest and certainly the star of the foreign contingent. Their lavish budget of £30,000 was attributed to the Czar's partiality for the Scots race and its history; less sentimentally it reflected strong trading connections between Scotland and Russia. The exhibit in the Industrial Hall concentrated on the recent development of the industrial resources of this 'sealed up European state'. But more appealing was the 'Russian Village' of six buildings in the grounds, including four magnificent pavilions for Forestry, Mining, Agriculture and the reception of the Czar, should he visit. The 180 Russians who built it

94 and 95. The French display in the Industrial Hall rested on the country's reputation for sophistication and consisted mainly of conventional 'art ware'.

96 and 97. The remarkable 'Russian Village' was the largest foreign exhibit. The strong colouring and extravagant forms of the timber buildings made a deep impression. Below, Shekhtel's drawings for the General and Agricultural Buildings.

entertained derisive onlookers with their primitive techniques and relaxed demeanour - they did almost everything with their axes, and very slowly, singing and smoking the while. But under the direction of the architect Shekhtel (an admirer of Mackintosh) these peasant carpenters erected complex buildings of stunning form and colouring (pale green, red, salmon, blue, with expanses of gilding and silvering). Their strange painted decorations were persistently mistaken for the work of the 'Glasgow School', according to one wit. From architectural critics who were baffled, if often impressed, they elicited words like 'bizarre', 'fantastic', 'outrageous', 'mad'.[13] The late opening of this ambitious scheme in mid-June

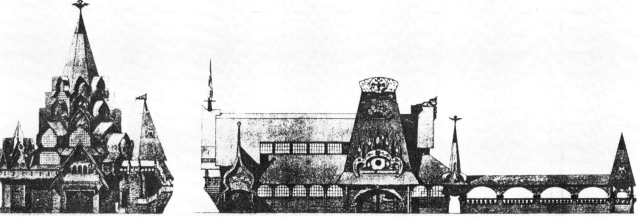

(after a strike by half the workmen over bad food, tea and pay - they were paid about a third of the Scottish rate before stoppages), was greeted as a welcome novelty, for already it was felt that the Exhibition was wearing thin on entertainment.

Two of Glasgow's leading firms had contributed picturesque structures in the grounds. Templeton's offered 'an opulent bit of colour and curious architecture', with its mosque-style pavilion between the white Industrial Hall and the brown Art Galleries. This made an effective home for a sumptuous display of carpets in all styles, from basic Oriental to modern designs by Walter Crane. Walter Macfarlane and Co., besides its impressive exhibit in the Machinery Hall, had erected the cast-iron Saracen Fountain, massive and elegant, on the main drive. Its design incorporated the twelve signs of the zodiac and lifesize figures of 'Art', 'Science', 'Literature', and 'Commerce' modelled by D. W. Stevenson, RSA. Near the Rockery Bandstand, this became a focal point of evening entertainments.

Another quaint building was a replica of a pair of the cottages erected by the soap manufacturers Lever Bros for the employees at Port Sunlight; it still stands in Kelvingrove Park. Since the Prince Consort built his artisans' dwellings at the Crystal Palace a paternalistic interest in the

98. Home-sick Russians were a subject of pitying interest. (*Bailie*)

99. The 'Sunlight' cottages reproduced the model accommodation (including bathrooms) erected for their workers by Lever Bros. They were given to the Corporation and still stand in Kelvingrove Park. (*ILN*)

living conditions of the working class had been displayed at many exhibitions, for example at Edinburgh in 1886 and Manchester in 1887. There had been nothing of this sort in 1888: despite a distinguished record in the provision of public services, Glasgow evidently shrank from drawing attention to the notoriously appalling housing and sanitation endured by its poorest citizens. As it was, the size and half-timbered style of the 1901 cottages belonged to another world. The norm in Glasgow was tenement dwellings.

Equally irrelevant, but with all the charm of the unfamiliar, was the Model Farm, with an ideal farm labourer's house and a full range of buildings. This was a novel idea and proved extremely popular. It was erected by Spiers and Co. to show off their constructions in iron and wood, and was equipped, in accordance with the industrial ethos of the exhibition, with the latest machinery. Cows and bees were withdrawn before opening, but the St Mungo Poultry Company, which was sensibly promoting egg production at a period when Britain was massively dependent on food imports, came forward with a poultry exhibit. The crowds round the incubators when chicks of all kinds, including swans, began to hatch showed what really fascinated city-dwellers. Connected with the farm was the Working Dairy: its iced, super-aerated, pasteurised milk was a popular summer refreshment. There was also a domed and tastefully stencilled Agricultural Building which made a central feature of the German Potash Syndicate's exhibit - a monumental sculpture from Paris which bestowed the prestige of art and allegory upon its product.

The most splendid building in the grounds was the Grand Concert Hall, seating more than 3000. It was unanimously conceded to be an improvement on the arrangements in 1888, when performances in the Grand Hall of the Main Building were disturbed by the tramp of feet on the wooden boards of the exhibit areas. Built in 'Venetian' style, with saucer dome, it was constructed on a double circle of columns, the outer 140 ft in diameter, the inner 115 ft, with a gallery created between them.

100. Inside the Grand Concert Hall with its gay scheme of decoration ('gaudy' to some eyes). Acoustics were unfortunately less impressive than the structure: there was a troublesome echo.

CONCERT HALL.

There were daily recitals on its electrically powered Grand Organ but the concert programme was regarded in some quarters as shamingly parochial. At the beginning of the season no big names had been engaged, nor any of the famous Yorkshire choirs - not even the Edinburgh choir, generally held to be Scotland's best. Much of the £20,000 music budget was allocated to band music, which could be heard throughout the afternoon and evening: a number of foreign bands, including Sousa's famous ensemble, lent some international class here.

Free music was a big selling point for the Exhibition, and partly responsible for the great increase in the number of season tickets sold - 55,000 before the opening, as compared with 12,000 in 1888. At one guinea they represented excellent value for a season's entertainment. Sales were up to 80,000 in early June, when the controversial question of charging extra for concerts was raised, as the scramble for seats had become impossible. There were also complaints that concerts were being used as a 'retreat for tired mothers with squalling infants'. Nursemaids and their charges were noticeable daytime attenders at this Exhibition. Charges were implemented and increased income did enable better bookings. Dame Nellie Melba was secured for three concerts in September: tickets for her were 2 shillings.

101 and 102. The Grand Concert Hall from the east; and below an allusion to the introduction of supplementary charges for concerts. (*Bailie*)

Cholly's grumble 3ᵈ Extra for Concert & only 2ᵈ left for car fares -

103. The Royal Bungalow restaurant, the Exhibition's best eating place, reflecting spectacularly in the river.

The vastly increased number of locals using the Exhibition as a summer amenity put a considerable strain on the facilities for refreshment. It was asserted that these were actually more limited than in 1888; certainly they were not much greater, an unfortunate miscalculation. Familiar complaints were levelled at the prices charged: these had been fixed by the Committee, and were defended as no greater than at other exhibitions. J. and W. McKillop were now in partnership with Mackenzie, and the firm again snared the sole contract to sell alcohol and ran another expensive 'oriental' Royal Bungalow, as well as the high-class Grosvenor, attached to the Concert Hall, and the Grand Avenue Buffet. McKillop's daily standing order makes impressive reading: 1600-1800 lbs of beef and mutton, 800-1000 lbs of fish, 4 tons of ice, 2 tons of potatoes, 600 bundles of asparagus, etc. Jenkins and Co. ran the 'popular', i.e. lower-class, Palace Restaurant and tea rooms: on a Wednesday in July between 4 and 7 pm they got through 265 dozen eggs and 35 hams. The large Prince's Restaurant, run by a London contractor, occupied the highest ground of the Exhibition and was prettily festooned with coloured lights.

Tea rooms had become a significant part of Glasgow's cultural life in the 1890s, thanks largely to the entrepreneurial flair of Kate Cranston, renowned as a discerning patron of Mackintosh. At the Exhibition her

FROM THE WEST.

large and tastefully decorated Tea House (the top floor an open, creeper-shaded Terrace Tea Garden) commanded the bridge built for the Exhibition opposite the Art Galleries. Flint's ran an elegant rival establishment, white with stencilled decoration, near the Concert Hall. Van Houten's made their mark again: this time they had abandoned national dress and given lavish carte blanche to local designers. Their 'Old English' pavilion was decorated by Guthrie and Wells and furnished by Wylie and Lochhead in Chippendale style, art blue and ivory. They offered a serviette, biscuit and Royal Worcester cup of cocoa at the reduced price of one penny.

From the beginning it was clear that the Executive had underestimated their fellow citizens' interest in amusement. Their high-minded but somewhat stuffy attitude, that 'the Exhibition is of itself important and interesting enough to exist without the doubtful aid of side-shows', was not shared by the general public, whose appetite for fun had been whetted in 1888. The most popular new attraction was the Canadian Water Chute, which had been operating successfully in London: the thrilling plunge into the Kelvin, quite an expensive treat at 6d a go, was described as a 'must'. There was also a miniature railway, built in the USA, which did a circuit round the Russian Village; and the Indian Theatre mentioned above. Otherwise the offerings were those tried and tested in 1888: the gondoliers were back, together with electric launches, and the

104 (*opposite*). A general view from the west, capturing the noble extent of the Industrial Hall. Miss Cranston's Tea House faces a newly constructed trestle bridge. Running by the river in the foreground is the much loved switchback railway.

105. The Kelvin was put to good recreational use and the gondola returned to Glasgow. Tranquillity was broken by the regular descent of the water chute into the river at a point just to the right of this picture.

Glaswegian's 'old friend' the switchback (all 3d); and the shooting jungle and rifle range at 1d. Penny-in-the-slot biographs were popular, especially when there was a topical disaster on show, like the dismasting in May of *Shamrock II*, the new Americas Cup challenger launched by Denny's for Sir Thomas Lipton only a month before.

Compared for instance with 1899's Greater Britain Exhibition at Earl's Court, with its spectacular show 'Savage South Africa' ('savages and horses' specially trained), its Crystal Maze, Opium Den, African Giantess, Electric Boy, and countless other attractions, Glasgow's Exhibition was positively austere. Private enterprise out of bounds saw the gap. The Scottish Zoo and Variety Circus supplied some side-show interest, and in June an entrepreneur opened 'The River', an aquatic panorama first produced in New York, which floated visitors past scenes of many lands. Why, asked *The Exhibition Illustrated* of 15 June, commenting on the 'crying need' for more entertainment at the Exhibition, was this 'harmless (and in its way instructive) show' outside the boundaries? From nothing at the Crystal Palace the amusement sections of exhibitions had expanded over the years, encouraged by the relentless demand for novelty, and shrewd recognition of public taste. In sticking to their idealistic concept of an exhibition, the Committee clearly miscalculated people's now vocal expectations of entertainment. As it was, the concessionaries did very well, with takings nearly three times those in 1888. The switchback claimed 1,111,000 passengers, the water chute 651,000.

The 'mania' for sports had reached a pitch which worried churchmen in the 1890s, and sporting events were an important part of the entertainment programme. Paris the year before had held the Olympic Games in conjunction with its Exposition (a pattern followed at St Louis 1904, and London 1908). A new stadium on the University grounds with banked cycle track and grandstand was used for the athletics and cycle-racing which were so popular at this period, and as a base for the novel automobile trials. It also provided for what had become the chief leisure interest of the Glasgow working man - football. Celtic played Rangers on the opening day. Other highlights included the Glasgow International Exhibition Regatta in June, a brave sight on the Clyde.

The Traffic and Excursion Committee had co-operated highly effectively as in 1888 with the railway companies and local steamship lines, which served all the world's major ports. An agent visiting major works with prices of excursion trains for parties of 200 or 500 was often successful, demonstrating that 'trades' unionism has not entirely killed the pleasant relations between employers and their workmen'.[14] Emigrants making the Exhibition an excuse to revisit their roots steamed home across the ocean. Conferences and congresses had become an important adjunct of major exhibitions, forwarding the ideal of the peaceful exchange of ideas among nations. Glasgow in 1901 had managed to make itself the venue for nearly all the important meetings of that year - the British Association for the Advancement of Science, Naval Architects in July (including a posse of Germans), and International Lawyers in August, the International Engineering Congress, and, a useful coup for the Executive, the International Association of Journalists. The Exhibition coincided also with the University's ninth jubilee celebrations, and students wandering the grounds in fancy dress were a colourful diversion in June.

For all the complaints, the city was proud of its 'X'. Once again Glaswegians had a shared experience, and they followed it avidly in the newspapers. Important visitors, like the Crown Prince of Siam, and the Empress Eugenie (who came incognito) caused a pleasant stir. There were sweepstakes on the attendance figures, and Exhibition romances to read about. Local japesters added more enlivenment - as when some apprentice boys booked up the dozen or so bath chairs and rode around in them to widespread dismay; then swooped on the Red Cross tent and its 'fine-lookin' nurse', where one of them leapt into the tidy bed. The weather was so unnaturally good that when Miss Cranston's establishment with its rooftop tea garden burnt down on 8 July the temporary marquee which was erected was felt to provide welcome shade. Band music floated on the air, and James Pain's firework shows (including treats like Performing Elephants, the Firework Blondin on a Tightrope and Fire Portraits of their Majesties) were magnificent. Illuminations switched on at the end of

106. Visiting engineers were offered trips to Aberfoyle, Lanark, Loch Lomond, Bute and Arran, Edinburgh and the Forth Bridge. The guide's cover shows a panorama of the site prepared from early plans: the two columns flanking a grand fountain, for example, never materialised.

107. Exhibition football matches catered for the Glasgow working man's ruling passion. (*Bailie*)

108. Illuminations turned the Exhibition into a 'fairyland': the Industrial Hall from the river.

109. 'When the Exhibition is no more.' Many marriages were made at Glasgow's Exhibitions. (*Bailie*)

BERTY KELVINHAW WILL WALK OUT THE 'NYCE GEL HE MET ET THE BEND' AND ROAM WHERE THE SEARCH-LICHT REIGNETH NOT.

August covered buildings with a tracery of white, red, green and amber lights, a breathtaking sight. At closing time the great Schuckert searchlight used at Paris and Chicago played over buildings and crowds, causing much merriment at the expense of courting couples.

Closing day when it came was rainy. Despite the best efforts of the 'seasons', the day's attendance of 173,266 was well below the 200,000 target, though the overall total of 11,497,220 (which could be generously rounded up to 13 million including free admissions for school children) was satisfactory. The dampening of spirits was seen in many quarters as further benevolence from heaven. Souvenir hunting, both legitimate and unauthorised, was fierce: everyone wanted a memento of the summer. But the police who had been anticipating rowdyism had little more than a broken window to report as the last visitors were shooed from the grounds. The show was over again, to almost everyone's regret.

The aftermath of an Exhibition was always depressing as magnificence was cleared away and remaining buildings grew dilapidated in the winter rains. But there was a good profit: the proceeds from auction of fittings and materials were set against the restoration of the Park, and the surplus was made over to the Art Purchase Fund for the further enhancement of Glasgow's now properly celebrated new Art Galleries.

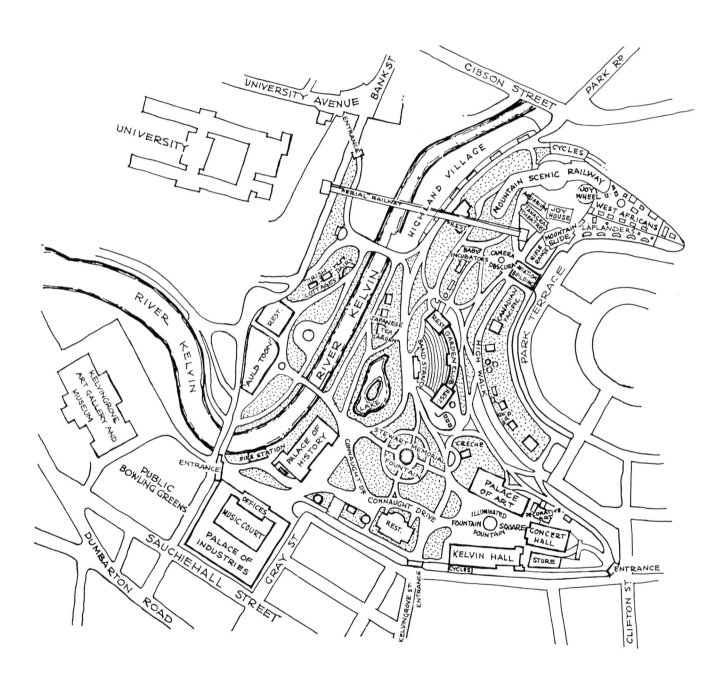

110. The Scottish Exhibition of National History, Art and Industry, 1911, held in Kelvingrove Park. (Based on the official plan.)

1911

Glasgow's International Exhibitions of 1888 and 1901 made a pair - expressions of the City's Victorian self-confidence, very similar in aims and arrangement, and successful enough to be hard to repeat. Something different was called for the next time round. The Scottish Exhibition of National History, Art and Industry staged in 1911, as another King, George V, awaited coronation, supplied it admirably. History displaced Industry, and the Exhibition's prominently stated aim .was to fund the endowment of a chair of Scottish History and Literature at Glasgow University. Behind it was the belief was that 'the time had fully arrived when Scottish history should be placed on a different plane from that which it had hitherto occupied in the education of the rising generations'.

111. The royal party arriving outside the Palace of History in a fleet of Argyll cars on opening day. The long white building on the hill is the Garden Club, and above the site is the handsome curve of Park Terrace.

Notes to this chapter appear on page 189.

Glasgow in its Victorian heyday has been compared to Venice, autonomous and outward-looking, as oblivious of Scotland as was Venice in her prime of Italy. Now, embracing patriotism, the Second City of Empire turned to develop its national identity and make an energetic bid for the cultural leadership of Scotland so casually exercised over the centuries by Edinburgh. As in 1888 a special spur was the desire to emulate, but on a much grander scale, a similar exhibition held in Edinburgh in 1908.

In retrospect the Exhibition's emphasis on the past and the narrower concerns of nationalism seems symptomatic of a dangerous economic conservatism and complacency. 1901 and the death of Queen Victoria had indeed marked the end of an era: in Glasgow's Edwardian years appeared clear signs of the troubles ahead. Local deposits of coal and ironstone were in decline, and the economy's reliance on specialised heavy industry and foreign markets was to prove fatal in a fast-changing world. In steel-making and engineering there were indications that the region's firms were adapting too slowly to modern advances - the crucial development of the marine diesel engine for instance was happening abroad. Serious foreign competition was undermining central industries like locomotive-building: the North British Locomotive Company was struggling, and in 1910 built only half its capacity of 600 locomotives. There was a shipbuilding slump from 1906-8, and the Argyll Motor Company, dogged by misfortune, was heading for liquidation. Labour unrest in docks, mines, railways and factories was brewing up to widespread strikes in 1911 and 1912.

112. The Exhibition's emblematic sticker, showing St Andrew's cross, the Scottish lion, and the tower of the Palace of Industry, which was the most recognisable building.

But Glasgow was used to cyclical depressions, and activity in the crucial shipyards had been boosted back to new heights by the naval race with Germany. There was too evidence of promising diversification, such as Beardmore's development of aero-engines. Prophesies of doom and accusations of nationalistic head-burying would have been dismissed out of hand by the prosperous citizens who flocked enthusiastically to Glasgow's grand new Scottish Exhibition. Devolution was the issue of the day. The focus of attention had shifted from civic to parliamentary politics, where the Scottish vote in 1910 had been largely responsible for confirming the Liberals in power. Scottish Liberals in Westminster were committed to devolution, and home-rule for Ireland was on the cards. With nearly a third of the cabinet Scots, or sitting for Scottish seats, independence seemed within reach. Political nationalism was complemented by a cultural renaissance, and things Gaelic, for so long suppressed, had become fashionable. Glasgow's Scottish Exhibition offered a timely focus for this resurgence.

What had begun as the idea of a 'few enthusiastic patriots' rapidly found wider support as a general appetite in the city for another really big show fixed upon the project.[1] The involvement of hard-nosed men of business was valuable, though it did lead to some conflicts of purpose. More general aims clustered around the early object of funding a new Chair: 'The Exhibition should be so designed as to create a greater public interest in Scottish History and Literature; should celebrate distinguished

113. The royal party in the Palace of Art. Left to right: the imposing Lord Provost, the Hon. Archibald McInnes Shaw; A. H. Pettigrew, Chairman of the Executive Council, later knighted for his efforts; the Duchess of Connaught and H.R.H. The Duke; the Marquis of Tullibardine, Hon. President of the Exhibition, and his Marchioness; the Duchess of Montrose; Thomas Dunlop, James Bell (both later knighted) and Patrick Dunn.

114. The Exhibition's Manager, W. H. Knight, was a busy man. (*Bailie*)

Scotsmen; and should represent a realistic picture of Scottish Burghal Life in bygone times, exhibiting those Arts and Industries in which the Scottish people are, or have been, pre-eminent, and encouraging Exhibits from all sources for comparison and instruction, and for the stimulation of national enterprise - due attention being given to Modern Art, Music and Out-Door Entertainment.'[2] The old aims of Victorian industrial exhibitions were added to something distinctively national and historical.

The snowballing ambitions of the enterprise for the first time created serious headaches for the organisers. With two days to go pressmen found steamrollers still levelling muddy roadways, while chaos reigned in the main exhibition halls. But somehow things were pulled together in time for the opening on 3 May 1911, which was unfortunately wretchedly wet.

A national exhibition pulled less rank than an international one. The opening was deputed to the King's uncle, the Duke of Connaught, while the King and Queen stayed in London to open the Festival of Empire at the Crystal Palace (rebuilt at Sydenham in 1854) on 12 May. The Duke's son, Prince Arthur of Connaught, opened the Coronation Exhibition at the Great White City six days later. Abroad there were international shows at Turin and Dresden. But on this occasion Glasgow, previously so sensitive to charges of parochialism, was free to exploit to the full the world's weakness for tartan and the romance of Scotland. The historical fancy-dress of the buildings and occupants gave the Exhibition a strong and widely appealing image. Although there were naturally those who remembered past glories and were disappointed, it was soon clear that Glasgow had pulled off another major success. An advertisement early in June claimed that 'The entire British press unanimously agree that nothing better in Exhibitions could be imagined or desired.' In fact despite

115. The main entrance gate, striking the firmly Scottish Baronial note which dominated the architecture of the Exhibition.

116 (*opposite*). The view from the top of the Grand Amphitheatre by the White Cockade restaurant down to the imposing tower of the Palace of Industry. On the right is the Palace of History, built round the remains of Kelvingrove Mansion.

its size, which was comparable with its International predecessors, the Exhibition's firmly nationalistic character led to its being largely ignored by the national, or rather London, press, both general and specialist. The impending Coronation was evidently of more interest to English readers.

Kelvingrove Park was used again and made a picturesquely appropriate setting for the Exhibition's Baronial main buildings, quaint Auld Toon and Highland Village. This time the site was pushed to the east end of the park, leaving the Museum and Art Gallery out of bounds. Since 1901 a new public road and bridge had bisected the park on the line of the last Exhibition's Grand Dome and ceremonial driveway, and a bowling green had replaced the west end of the Industrial Hall.

The trend towards dispersal of exhibits in numerous structures was carried further in 1911, with separate buildings, some dignified as 'Palaces', for History, Industry, Art, Electrical and Engineering exhibits (Kelvin Hall), Music, and Decorative Arts, together with numerous minor pavilions and kiosks. In contrast to the Oriental extravaganzas of 1888 and 1901, which had made no concessions to Scottish styles, 1911 sought a strong national image. This was most effectively captured in the Palace of History, modelled on Falkland Palace. Liberal application of turrets and crow-steps gave a loosely 'Baronial' effect to the other major buildings. But finished in white plaster, relieved by roofs of red and grey and green, they still impressed people as 'so many palaces of Aladdin'.

The minor buildings included many interesting structures, though there were architectural critics who complained that 'the prevalence of a too riotous fancy mars the general effect'.[3] They were generally discontented with the insufficient rigour of the layout - no proper axes, and undue regard for existing pathways, features and trees. The peculiar shape and demanding contours of the site indeed posed difficult problems, but were productive too of grand effects. The general public was inclined to find the whole arrangement agreeably scenic.

In the Palace of History and its vast collection of relics the educational purpose which motivated this Exhibition found its purest expression, disentangled from commercial interests. Mindful perhaps of the success of 1888's Bishop's Palace, the architect R. J. Walker[4] had created a fake historical building, not an exact replica this time, but based on the Palace of Falkland, once the seat of Scottish kings, with additional elements from the façade of Holyrood Palace. This was actually built round the remains of Kelvingrove Mansion, which since its use as the Japanese pavilion in 1901 had housed the Jeffery Library. The structure was of steel frame and asbestos boarding, with cement flooring, and no artificial heating or lighting was permitted for fear of fire. Fibrous plaster mouldings were used to good effect as in 1901. Finished in cement with grey slate roof, the palace looked quite authentic, while its rectangular shape accomodated six spacious galleries.

1888 had assembled a large and notable archaeological and historical collection, most of which had been produced again in 1901. But in 1911, Professor John Glaister and his sub-committees were attempting something to surpass all earlier displays. They had set themselves to the exhaustive categorisation of all Scottish historical relics, in the way that earlier exhibitions categorised all natural and manufactured products. Scottish History and Literature was divided into 34 sub-groups, and Ethnographical and Historical Objects into 24; while the Historical Portraits section assembled on a scale never attempted before the likenesses of famous men of Scotland over a period covering approximately James III (1451-88) to Sir Walter Scott (1771-1832).

The result was a collection of thousands of items which 'call up memories of kings and peasants, peace and war'. Some 1400 owners (including King George, who was said to be, like his grandmother, 'immensely interested' in his Scots ancestry) had contributed pieces with an insured

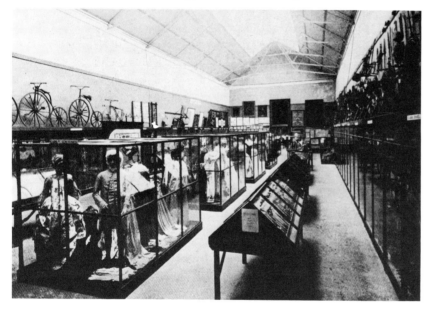

117. Serried ranks of cases in the East Gallery of the Palace of History. An attempt was made to present the material accessibly, but the quantity alone was overwhelming.

118. One of the aims of the Exhibition was to educate the young in their Scottish heritage. (*Bailie*)

value of £459,000. Among them were the most sacred objects of the Scottish race - a complete set of the charters of the Scottish kings; the letters of Sir William Wallace; the sword of King Robert the Bruce and the Brooch of Lorne dragged from him on the battlefield in 1306; a full array of Queen Mary and Bonnie Prince Charlie relics; an 'exceptionally complete' display of Robert Burns and Sir Walter Scott. The hope expressed in the *Official Catalogue* was that such exhibits 'will keep alive, in the breasts of all who reverently look upon them, the love of their native land - the ancient kingdom of Scotland - and will sustain affection for those who have made their nation's history "that makes her lov'd at home, revered abroad"'. These things did arouse emotion. An outraged correspondent early complained that the precious relics were apparently unguarded: Queen Mary's cradle was being rocked by careless passers by (and worse, laughed at as old-fashioned); and don't our 'American cousins' have a reputation for helping themselves to chips of various objects of note?

Such was the scope of the collection that some parts of it were late opening: a Cornishman who had travelled up expressly to see the prehistoric section was understandably cross. The giant catalogue of 1155 pages, no ephemeral volume, did not finally appear until mid August, after months of 'next week' promises. It cost two shillings and its weight attracted much comment: 'Thank goodness that yin's away ... I've been humphin' it aboot all day, and it has nearly paralysed one of my arms' (a programme lad in the heat). 'Its handsome blue cover', thought one wit, 'will match the blue stockings seen in such profusion'. A *de luxe* illustrated edition was also published.

Emphasis was laid on the contribution of concrete displays to the 'vivification' of history. Although display techniques seem rudimentary to modern eyes, there was some high-minded effort to make the material accessible to ordinary people and 'educative to the willing learner': school parties were frequent visitors. The prehistoric section, for example, bigger than ever before, included a full-size statue of a 'Typical Man of Stone Age' and models of bronze age huts to bring to life this remotest period of Scotland's past. Elsewhere attempts were made to link portraits with cases of the personal belongings which have always exercised an irresistible fascination - Mary Queen of Scots' scissors, Flora Macdonald's slippers, Bonnie Prince Charlie's baby rattle. Other sections showed material of social significance - domestic utensils, clothing and so on. Juxtaposition was often peculiar: adjacent to each other in the catalogue are for instance 'Valentine section, Armada relics, Burghal relics, The Roman section, Furniture section' (South Gallery); or 'Robert Owen and New Lanark, Mary Queen of Scots etc., Gretna Green Marriages, Jacobite Literature' (Mid Gallery). A large collection of weapons evoked the stirring and often bloody past, in particular the patriotic struggle against English domination, represented by Covenanting swords and pistols, and the Jacobite relics of '15 and '45.

Important historical relations between Scotland and Sweden, Norway and the Netherlands were dealt with in separate sections, and ties of friendship renewed by official visitors to the Exhibition, including the Crown Prince and Princess of Sweden in July. The old alliance with France was also represented, though owing to 'recent history' the number of exhibits was less than the importance of the relationship warranted. In flaunting these ties with the continent Scotland further enhanced its sense of distinctness from England.

A new bridge over the Kelvin just north of the Palace of History led visitors to the past less accurately but more appealingly vivified in a bogus Auld Toun, or Olde Toun, put together to be 'characteristic of quaint bits of our older Scottish architecture' and inhabited by picturesquely attired burghers. Such features had proved very popular at past exhibitions, for example 'Old Edinburgh' in 1886 and 'Old Manchester and Salford' in 1887; but Glasgow, which did not live much in the past and had in fact

119. The Keep outside the Auld Toon was cunning camouflage for the Saracen Fountain, which was later moved to Alexandra Park.

120 (*opposite*). The Main Square of the Auld Toon, with mercat cross, town crier, Auld Tartan Shop and Olde Toffee Shoppe. There is a strong foretaste of Disneyland in this evocation of a quaint burghal past.

destroyed most of it, had not previously cared to take up the idea. The Toon was composed of a generic Old Castle Keep (which ingeniously disguised the Saracen fountain given to the city after 1901), and more or less accurate replicas of a 'Typical Scottish Town Hall', modelled on Dunbar Town Hall, and assorted Glasgow buildings, most of them now gone: St Ninian's Chapel (which housed the Girls' Club for female attendants), Old Gorbals Tower, and houses from Stockwell St, Gorbals, Tiddler's Close (High St), and Rottenrow. There was a harsh irony in the demolition later this year, after a fire, of the old Tontine House in the Trongate, one of the few vestiges of real Old Glasgow.

This 'romantic little township nestling in the heart of Kelvingrove' did not have much to do with historical reality. It was a charming sham, constructed of wood, plaster and canvas, so cunningly painted that there was even the semblance of moss upon the walls. Such was the 'realism' that delighted visitors. This 'quiet, old-world nook, with its towering turrets, its crow steps and its toppling chimneys, just so much awry as to

accentuate the verisimilitude of it all, is a place apart, a spot to which one may retire from the din and ecstasy of the coming summer nights and recall the picturesque and historic past'.[5] In fact as the less poetic pointed out, to achieve this one needed to block out the hum of the scenic railway, the plump of soda-water bottles, hobble skirts and flannel suits. But most visitors were more than ready to succumb to sentimental nostalgia for 'days gone forever in Scotland'. They enjoyed buying their souvenirs, not so rigorously in period as to exclude the new Teddy bears[6] from quaintly garbed inhabitants in the olde worlde shoppes. This consumer-oriented, trim and tidy 'living history' concept has proved enormously successful in

121 and 122 (*left*). Two postcards: the Auld Toon in coloured tartan frame, and picturesquely attired inhabitants outside Bailie Nicol Jarvie's Shop.

123. Miss Agnes Bartholomew as Mary Queen of Scots in one of the Exhibition's historical plays: she 'looked and played it to the life'.

the twentieth century, as is demonstrated by recreations like Williamsburg in the USA and the historic features in the countless Theme Parks descended from Disneyland.

Pageants, which offered 'living history' in a different guise, were currently in vogue: several were being performed in London as part of the Festival of Empire. At Glasgow it was decided that 'These Living Pictures and Demonstrations will be of such a character as to appeal to the patriotism of Scotsmen in a marked degree'. Neil Munro was to have written a Jacobite pageant, but backed out at a late stage in the face of a dispute with his lady producer. Sir George Douglas' drama in blank verse on Robert the Bruce, with special music from the Aeolian Ladies' Orchestra and pipes in the last act, was however a considerable popular and financial success. So too were the Burns and Queen Mary plays by George Eyre Todd, secretary to the Historical section, which played to packed audiences and made a handsome profit of £700.[7] But the Burns pageant especially attracted indignant criticism from some quarters. The scene in which the poet was brought back drunk and dying from the Globe Tavern was regarded as an especially monstrous vilification of a national hero: 'There is apparently much need of a chair of Scottish History'. The Pageant of Glasgow Cross and Castle by the Rev. James Primrose was likewise berated as 'unhistorical' and 'music-hall', and particular exception was taken to the Bishop's papist tonsure.

The historical pageant treatment was also applied to some of the ship models which had featured so notably in Glasgow's previous Exhibitions. The centenary of 'one of Glasgow's greatest achievements', the building at Port Glasgow of the first commercially viable steam-vessel, Henry Bell's *Comet*, was ample excuse. Ship models had been arranged chronologically, starting with the *Comet*, in 1901, but the 1911 display took a longer and more imaginative view. The Kelvin came into its own as a series of historic vessels took to the water in a daily pageant, headed in warm weather by an ancient Briton 'clad in woad stain and little else, demon-

124 and 125. The *Victory* was among the historic model vessels which sailed in daily pageant on the Kelvin. Nos 12 and 15 in the photograph were the *Resolution*, a first-class cruiser of the type in use in 1887, and a modern Super Dreadnought. Warship orders were sustaining the Clyde shipyards at this period. On the bank can be seen pavilions erected by Cailler's (chocolate) and Chiver's (marmalade etc.), and the Japanese Tea House.

FITTING UP THE VICTORY

strating the navigation of the coracle'. A Scottish angle was zealously sought: no. 4 for instance, a fourteenth-century ship, was billed as 'The type of vessel probably built by King Robert the Bruce in his days of retirement at Cardross on Clyde'; and no. 7, a Spanish galleass, 'The type of ship of the Spanish Armada which lies at the bottom of Tobermory Bay'. Last in the line came the latest productions of the Clyde shipyards. Unlucky no. 13 was the giant liner *Lusitania*, launched by John Brown in 1907 for Cunard, later to be torpedoed, on 7 May 1915, on its way from New York to Liverpool. Ominously bringing up the rear were no. 14, a torpedo boat destroyer, and no. 15, a Super-Dreadnought battleship.

The Palace of Industry, clothed in Scottish Baronial grandeur, was not the Exhibition's most important building on this occasion, but it was the largest. Its high tower was immediately recognisable and became the Exhibition's key image. The Palace occupied the site of the east end of the 1901 Industrial Hall, and squashed within three public roads and set back

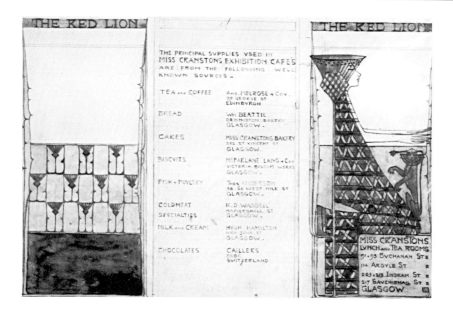

126 and 127. The doyenne of Glasgow's tea rooms, Miss Cranston, ran the Red Lion café overlooking the Music Court of the Palace of Industry. Frances Macdonald designed the menu (her sister Margaret did the card for Miss Cranston's other Exhibition establishment: see 136). Clients taking tea on the balcony could enjoy music performed below - here by the pipers of the Scottish Horse.

128 (*opposite*). The Court was dominated by the fine tower of the Palace of Industry, which became the key image of the Exhibition.

from the main site, it did not dominate the grounds as its much larger predecessors had done. The number of exhibitors was much smaller overall - there were approximately 640, divided between the Palace of Industry, Kelvin Hall, Auld Toon and grounds. But if on this occasion industry had lost its prime importance, the commercial aspect of the Exhibition was nevertheless crucial to its viability.

There was an attempt to make the building partially self-contained by designing it to enclose an arcaded Music Court, a 'dream of beauty' in the evenings with its palms and fairy lights, with a balcony for refreshments run by Miss Cranston above. The north side housed offices and banking facilities in a separate block. Above them was a conference hall provided

with an eye to attracting the annual meetings of various societies and associations, which were a useful contribution to any exhibition's prestige and cash flow. Planning of the 1911 buildings was altogether very well thought through. The Palace of Industry was temporarily retained after the close to house the Scottish Motor Exhibition, and led to the construction of the predecessor of the present Kelvin Hall as a permanent exhibition venue for Glasgow.

Architectural critics champing for more order overall found the arrangements within too riotously laissez-faire. 'It seems unfortunate that in a scheme of this kind each exhibitor should be allowed to work his own happy or unhappy fancy in the design of his stall.'[8] Although 14 classes of exhibit were announced in the catalogue, no clear order was observable in the listing or on the floor. Glendinning's Beevinalt medicated wine food, for instance, was showing back to back with nitrate of soda for explosives. Foreign participants - from Austria, Denmark, Holland, Germany, Italy, Japan - appeared here and there adding material sophistication to the displays. Features like 'Orientals' weaving Saraband rugs and carpets in an Eastern temple were popular as ever. Thomas Cook (next to Sideroleum wood preservative) was giving space to Canadian and Victorian government exhibits and assisting as emigration broker. A number of railway companies and shipping lines were exhibiting here, among them Cunard, showing a complete first-class stateroom.

Again no sales were permitted without special permission. Firms might take orders but 'shall not sollicit them to the annoyance of the public or other Exhibitors'. Catalogue listings often adopted the language of advertisements. Exhibiting to the trade was less significant than it had been in 1888 and 1901 and manufacturers were clearly concentrating on appealing to the consumer. The Carron Company, for example, which made a wide range of cast-iron products, restricted its main display to two bays of firegrates and a fitted bathroom (though it showed steamships on another stand). Bathrooms, the key to middle class status, were generally much in evidence. Shanks of Barrhead showed four, but was trumped by its rival Doulton, with six complete bathrooms for all tastes. No. 1 offered every essential of the modern bathroom, 'in substantial make and pleasing design', for £12; while no. 3, with silver-plated fittings and green onyx basin top, would cost 'well over £100'. As in 1888 Doulton had also installed all the Exhibition lavatories in its latest patterns, a useful practical advertisement. (Shanks had done 1901.)

Appeal to the feminine temperament was marked throughout. A wide range of domestic appliances could be inspected - vacuum cleaners, hygienic glass washers, the Acme Ice-Cream freezer. The Glasgow department stores were showing in force, none more prominently than Pettigrew and Stephens. Immediately inside the entrance, vying with the large stand of the Scottish Co-operative Wholesale Society, was its glamorous display of gowns. Elsewhere the firm showed the manufacture of its proprietary 'Wooltex' underwear, 'so favourably known at home and abroad', and on another stand the weaving of P. & S. Scotch Wincey, 'as supplied

129. Exhibits in the Palace of Industry were fewer than in 1888 and 1901 but included much to attract the consumer. (*Bailie*)

to Queen Alexandra'. A fourth display promoted its own-brand 'Torch' tableware. Among working exhibits Stewart and Young's confectionery was again especially popular with the ladies.

The absence of a separate Women's Section is noteworthy after the prominent place it took in 1888 and 1901. In 1911 it was apparently felt that the Suffragettes were making quite enough trouble already and did not need any encouragement. Women's efforts were instead supposed to be generally diffused throughout the Exhibition: a Ladies' Committee of 101 plus two secretaries had no obvious function. Most committees remained all male, but women were given a voice in matters deemed suitable: 7 out of 18 members of the Pageants Committee were female, and the Highland Village had a 'large and intellectual committee of ladies'. Miss Frances Melville, MA, headed a committee organising lectures on 'Callings for Women', which kept alive in peripheral form the aspirations of the earlier Women's Sections. There were no fripperies like the 'Fair of Fashion' at the Festival of Empire. The only exclusively female province was a committee headed by Mrs Pettigrew for the 'Welfare of Women and Girls', which organised lodging and ran a club on the lines of that established in 1901 for the numerous female attendants. Once again the Exhibition was a heavy employer of women, and the attraction of a summer's waitressing in the heart of things led to complaints of a dearth of domestic servants.

Feminine talents in craft and design which had previously formed the core of the Women's Art and Industries section were however given a proper place in a separate building devoted to the Decorative and Ecclesiastical Arts. The convener was unusually a woman, Miss Story,

130. The somewhat undistinguished interior of the Decorative and Ecclesiastical Arts Building, where Scottish designers and Schools of Art displayed some first-class work. Many of the exhibitors here were women.

and serving on the committee were others connected with the Glasgow School of Art, Jessie Newbery and Ann Macbeth. Decorative Arts in 1901 had been housed inconspicuously in the Fine Art Section. Though small and hardly prominent, tucked into the corner between the Palaces of

Music and Fine Arts, the building represented overdue recognition of a field in which Glasgow boasted special distinction. At the same time its segregation from the main Industrial Arts building perhaps signified in concrete form an unfortunate weakening of the close links between Art and Industry which had been so powerfully urged by Fra Newbery and others at the end of the last century. The Edinburgh College of Art had one of the alcoves ranged round the central hall, but local talent was understandably dominant, to the extent that the building seemed 'almost an annexe' of the Glasgow School of Art and the Glasgow Society of Lady Artists. Among the individuals exhibiting were William Meikle, John Guthrie, Phoebe Traquair, Jessie King, George Logan, Kellock Brown, M. de Courcy L. Dewar (Miss), A. N. Paterson, Ann Macbeth and Talwin Morris.

The Fine Art Section was as ever prestigious, and occupied a building constructed like the Palaces of History and Music on a steel skeleton, with careful regard for the fireproofing of the valuable exhibits. A sculpture hall, seven galleries of oils and one each of watercolours, black and white, architecture and photography represented a century of Scottish Art. The span from Raeburn to the present was chosen to avoid a clash with the considerable number of paintings in the Historical Section, but also covered Scotland's main period of artistic achievement and development. Paintings ranged in style 'from the intense particularisations of William Dyce to the, as some hold, "anarchic" sketchiness of Mr S. J. Peploe, from the earnest, if mistakenly laboured, "messages" of Sir Noel Paton to the graciously distinctive utterances of Sir James Guthrie, from the prose of Sam Bough ... to the light, wind-and-sea animated poetry of McTaggart'.[9] Scottish origin was the qualification, though an exception was made for the immensely popular Sam Bough, judged 'a Scot by adoption'. This was a chance to reclaim painters like David Wilkie, Dyce, Orchardson and Pettie who had gone south and were often treated as 'English' painters. The Glasgow Boys were now part of the establishment: of the four who painted pictures for the dome in 1888, Guthrie and Walton now lived in Edinburgh, Lavery and Henry in London.

Facing the Palace of Art and matching it architecturally, though constructed on a conventional wooden frame, was the indirectly named Kelvin Hall. This housed Electrical and Engineering exhibits, a diminished form of the Machinery Section which had been the pride of Glasgow's first two Exhibitions but was now of minor significance (the Duke bypassed it on his opening tour). The substitution of name was obviously felt to add dignity and could be justified by the Exhibition's commitment to celebrating famous Scotsmen. The Central Hall was devoted to loan exhibits. A statue of Lord Kelvin (d. 1907) presided over a collection of apparatus associated with him, including a section of the Atlantic cable laid in 1857, and the bell-push used by Queen Victoria to switch on her Diamond Jubilee London illuminations in 1897, as well as many far more mysterious instruments. It was recognised that 'many will fail to understand the extreme value of many of the exhibits in the collection'. Neigh-

"WHIT'S WRANG WI' THE CAT, MAW? HUS IT GOT A FISH BANE IN IT'S THROAT?"

131. Fierce plaster lions adorned the Palace of Art (opposite). (*Bailie*)

132. On the left is the Palace of Art. The Concert Hall, or Palace of Music, commanded this part of the site, its high tower echoing that of the Palace of Industry. The Decorative Arts Building is in the corner between the two.

bouring displays of ship paintings and the Scottish National Antarctic Expedition aboard the *Scotia* were more accessible if less significant. That rarefied Science should thus oust the economically important heavy industry from its place in public esteem was in keeping with the cultural aspirations of this Exhibition, but indicative too of the growing hold of attitudes associated with Britain's economic decline. Certainly the practical enthusiasms of Glasgow's Victorian industrialists were often attenuated by southern refinement in the offspring who inherited their businesses.

The aim of this part of the Exhibition was 'to illustrate the progress of Electrical and Engineering Discovery and Invention, and the development of Electricity as an applied science'. In the commercial part of the hall the firm of Kelvin and White, originally established in 1859 and still successfully exploiting Lord Kelvin's pioneering scientific work, was showing navigational and electrical instruments. Scotland had been given a good start in this important area of light industry and by the twentieth century was manufacturing electrical appliances of all descriptions. But

despite this progressive emphasis on electrical engineering it was still the shipbuilding section which dominated general interest. Many fine old models appeared again, alongside those of more up-to-date ships, as the dockyards paraded their now historic development. Denny's , the pioneer of steel ships, led with a display contrasting early and modern examples of various classes of vessel - the paddle steamer *Loch Lomond* of 1845, for example, alongside the *Queen Alexandra* built in 1902 for Turbine Steamers Ltd. Yarrow had moved from the Thames to the Clyde in 1908, and now, busy on destroyers for the Admiralty, was exhibiting as a local.

The Concert Hall or Palace of Music, between the matching Palace of Art and Kelvin Hall, closed the vista at the south east corner of the site with its fine 120 ft tower, echoing the Palace of Industry. This was the only significant attempt at architectural layout on the site. The square thus enclosed accommodated 13,000 and was dominated by the descendant of 1888's Fairy Fountain, sorely missed in 1901. With a diameter of 50

133. The other side of the square in front of the Concert Hall, showing on the right the august Kelvin Hall, which faced the Palace of Art and was its architectural twin. This spot was particularly popular at night when the illuminated Fairy Fountain was in action.

feet it was not bigger than its predecessor, but it was trusted that the technical advances in this brilliant form of hydromechanics would be readily appreciated. 300 gallons of water a minute were illuminated by 20,000 candle power, 'a veritable charm at night'.

The Hall's rectangular interior was less daring than 1901's domed circle, but had the not inconsiderable advantage of decent acoustics. Its elegant white and gold décor and tip-up seats were widely approved. The proscenium had been designed with an eye to pageants, tableaux and receptions, as well as the concert programme, which was inaugurated by Sir Henry Wood and his Queen's Hall Orchestra on 3 May. Among other musical celebrities to grace the platform was Fritz Kreisler in September.

Miscellaneous exhibits were strung out along the High Walk leading from this corner of the Exhibition up to the flagstaff which marked the highest point of the grounds and the beginning of the entertainments area. First of note was the Arboricultural Pavilion, exhibiting rustic houses and the like, and a well-equipped apiary where 'the latest hints on Bee Culture can be obtained'. The German Potash Syndicate, the only serious representative of Germany in 1901, returned with an individual pavilion, and acetylene gas was again being urged upon the public, this time by Paterson's. The Scottish Red Cross Society had set up a camp.

The Caledonian Railway and the Canadian Pacific Railway were vying with each other in offering cinematographic journeys to an enthusiastic public. The latter had put up a structure in the tradition of North American exhibitions which was rather stuffily judged 'interesting' but perhaps too exuberant in detail with 'a questionable use of engine fronts as a decorative detail'. The company was also giving information on passages

134. Caricature American commandeering one of the bath chairs which were available at this and the earlier Exhibitions. (*Bailie*)

135. The exuberant Canadian Pacific pavilion, featuring engine fronts with cowcatchers and relief carving of harvest riches. Inside were paintings illustrating the theme of the Scot in Canada, and the chance of a cinematographic journey across the continent.

and prospects in Canada, which was absorbing Scots at around 17,000 a year as the tide of emigration swelled again.

The Aviation Pavilion, appropriately occupying the highest ground, had been erected free of charge by Spiers and Co., who had built the popular Farm in 1901. (The company also provided a model Crèche near the Palace of Art, where six lucky infants were supervised by a committee of ladies while their parents toured the grounds.) With its latest types of flying machines, full-scale and model, it appealed to the current craze for aviation and offered something excitingly modern, though its walls showed 'several very historical pictures dealing with the early history of aviation'. National colour came from a survey of Scottish progress in the field, from the glider flown in 1895 by Pilcher (whose untimely death in 1899 lost Glasgow an important innovator) to machines recently built in Glasgow and Stirling. But like mass car production in Scotland this bold

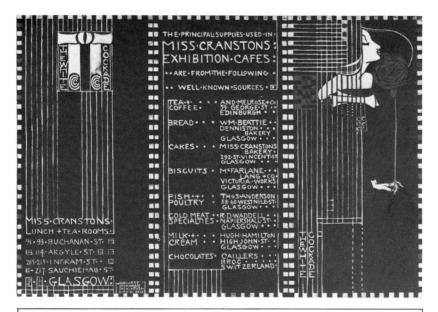

136 and 137. The menu card for Miss Cranston's White Cockade tea rooms, a telling design by Margaret Macdonald, the wife of Charles Rennie Mackintosh. Her sister Frances designed the card for Miss Cranston's Red Lion Café (126).

138. Tea on the balcony overlooking the Exhibition at the White Cockade. Miss Cranston had been for some time a discriminating patron of the 'Glasgow Style': Mackintosh designed the interior of this tea room for her.

attempt at diversification in the engineering industry was doomed to founder. Near the pavilion were the photographic studios of T. & R. Annan, once again official Exhibition photographers; and 'one of Oxo's characteristic exhibits'.

From the heights one looked from behind at the Exhibition's central feature, the Grand Amphitheatre designed for open-air band concerts, sheltered above by the elegant Garden Club and colonnades extending in a curve to two large restaurants on either hand, Miss Cranston's unlicensed White Cockade and McKillop and Sons' licensed Grosvenor - for the two major caterers of 1901 had again secured the prime contracts. The Garden Club had filled its list of 1000 privileged members at 2 guineas apiece well before the building was completed. Many people were put out by this élitism at the heart of the Exhibition. The masses were deprived of the pleasure of inspecting Royal Reception Rooms since there were none on this occasion: the Duke had been entertained at the Club on his visit by 'the 700 from Pollokshields, the 200 from Paisley, and the 100 from God knows where'.[10] When 200 or so additional places were advertised in early June there was another scramble for membership.

The Garden Club's dining and tea rooms (including a Ladies' Dining Room) were asserted by some to offer the only decent food in the Exhibition. Complaints of 'food fit only for a hungry schoolboy' - stale bread and butter, coarse scones and unattractive cakes at double price - were registered by the disgruntled. But Miss Cranston found her loyal champions. After the miscalculations of 1901 the space allocated to refreshments was ample, though perhaps excessively dominated by McKillop, who was once more the sole licensed contractor. Besides its amphitheatre restaurant the firm ran a three-storey restaurant overlooking the Stewart Memorial Fountain (trusting in another good Exhibition summer this

139. The Garden Club (members only) had a magnificent site above the Grand Amphitheatre and Bandstand.

140. Band music remained staple entertainment and was well provided for (a coloured postcard).

incorporated a roof garden in the manner of Miss Cranston's 1901 tea rooms) and a large establishment in a prime position on the west bank next to the Auld Toon. The 'popular' Carlton restaurant run by W. and R. S. Kerr was in the amusement area.

Music and entertainment on a scale never excelled in Scotland were advertised in 1911. Lavish provision was made for the ever popular bands (pipe bands were featured, but not as often as might have been expected). The spectacular Grand Amphitheatre had seating for 10,000. On the Auld Toon side of the river was another bandstand and amphitheatre, designed to be handed over to the Corporation after the close. Learning from the mistakes of 1901 and needing to keep up with the escalation of the 'funfair' content of exhibitions, the Executive had allowed a substantial amusement zone at the north end of the Park. Here Glaswegians could at last enjoy some of the thrills and side-shows long commonplace in London. Such attractions had become not only a financial necessity but also an important outlet for 'bigger and better' boasts, and Glasgow was offering all the 'latest developments', enthusiastically described in the *Official Guide*. Glasgow's proven success in staging exhibitions encouraged contractors to invest substantially in concessions.

The Mountain Scenic Ride, brought from the White City, was nearly a mile long, the most recent improvement on switchback, figure eight and

"IN REPLY TO YOUR GENEROUS ENCORE"
THE IDOL
AT THE GLASGOW EXHIBITION.

dip-of-the-dips rides, and 'surpasses by far anything of the kind previously built'. It was an immediate success and subject to long queues. Reproduced from the successful model at Brussels, the Mountain Slide, with two tracks and elevator, was a 'great advance on older forms of Helter Skelter and Slip Towers'. There was a new Tumbling Ride called Niagara Falls; and the 'Mysterious River', offering 'romance for youths and maidens' - the latest version of the River ride which had operated out of bounds in 1901. The Joy Wheel had been all the rage last season; the Joy House or Hall of Illusions was a longer established attraction. Other stand-bys were an old-fashioned camera obscura, and jungle and military

141. A postcard showing the Mountain Scenic Railway and the entrance to Mysterious River Rides.

142. The rides in the amusements section were especially popular with courting couples (a coloured postcard).

rifle ranges, but new in this last category was a cinematographic target. A genuine novelty was the Aerial Railway invented by W. L. Hamilton of Glasgow: the excitement of flying could be mildly experienced in a journey across the river 130 ft up in a car suspended from a metal 'balloon' electrically propelled along cables (there had been a number of 'dirigible' accidents recently, so it was important to stress the safety of this gasless mock airship).

Quieter pleasures were offered by a 'Tanagra Theatre', its representation of living characters 'a never ending source of marvel and delight', and an aquarium pretending to embody both entertainment and education, but erring on the safe side with stalactites, fairy lights and 'only marine life of the most peculiar and uncommon types'. A curious example of a freak show in heavy educational disguise was a Baby Incubator Institute, director M. Ehrlich, complete with premature babies. This in fact featured as an attraction at a number of exhibitions.

'Uncivilised' peoples and their strange habits also had the drawing power of freaks. Displays of the living human being in his native habitat were often justified as educational, but the usual location of these 'exhibits' in the amusement area, as at Glasgow, identified the real attraction. These shows were well established in the competitive London exhibitions: the Greater Britain Exhibition of 1899, for example (already referred to in

connection with 1901) featured Kaffir Kraals inhabited by 200 or so assorted Matabele, Swazi and Basuto, 'a source of boundless interest and amusement to visitors'. (This exhibition also had baby incubators.) Glasgow's representatives of the simple life were juxtaposed Arctic and Equatorial settlements, provided by Erhlich and Singer of London, who were also concessionaries for the Mountain Slide and Joy House. From the time that the natives arrived and were taken on a 'tour of inspection' round the city in wagonettes they proved a source of inexhaustible fascination and one of the Exhibition's major attractions. Shortly after they were settled into their huts they were inspected by a Medical Officer who pronounced all the 'inmates' to be in good health.

On one side Laplanders could be observed living 'in a most primitive fashion', with wives, children, reindeer and dogs. These simple people had apparently been 'easily persuaded to leave their homes' by the promise of as much milk as they wanted. The reindeer were destined for the zoo in Regent's Park after the Exhibition: how the unfortunate humans survived this experience is not related. The West Africans, about a hundred in all, assembled from Equatorial Africa, the French Congo, Dahomey and Sudan, were more entertaining to the crowds because they wore bright clothes and put on performances of singing, dancing and religious rites. Black people were indeed regarded as inherently uninhibited and

143 (*opposite*). 'Flying across the Kelvin' in a 'dirigible' towards the University silhouetted in the background. Below can be seen the Carlton restaurant and the cottages of the Highland Village. (*ILN*)

144. Laplanders in the 'Arctic Village' within the amusement area.

amusing. A visitor's offer of 6d for the sensation of kissing a black girl was accepted to shrieks of delight: 'There is no coyness about the African maiden'.

The *Souvenir of a Visit to the West African Colonies*, a pamphlet produced for visitors, is tellingly illustrative of the attitudes behind this sort of exhibit. Ostensibly serious and ethnographic, it begins with a survey of the area in terms of the natural resources valuable to its colonial proprietors, commenting in passing on the wasteful habits of native farming. There follows an account of the principal races. The Ouolofs, or Giolofs or Iolofs, are the 'darkest and best looking of the tribes. They are tall and well made; have woolly hair, wear beards, and cut their whiskers ... They are hardy, courageous, but with little foresight, and live only for pleasure.' The Mandigues or Malinkos are 'of medium height; vigorous and of different types, but the characteristics of the negro exist in all of them ... They are very agile and enterprising, and trade into the Sudan, and from there bring back slaves.' 'The Sousous have a dark brown skin, the nose is flat, the hair frizzly' and so on.

The simple arrangements of these primitive people 'not yet used to our mode of living' were a source of general interest. There was the usual entertainment to be had from observing the village artisans at work - the weaver, the jeweller remarkable for what he could do with such rudimentary tools, the cobbler who could turn a goat into charming slippers in no time, the cook 'whose black hands, however, make one feel a little dubious as to the cleanliness of the food - Rest Assured it is a Fast Colour'. Mealtimes were another spectacle: the natives eat with their fingers so naturally that 'one is highly amused, not shocked'. As to the dancing displays, the reader is assured that 'Decency is Maintained Throughout'. There is finally the question of the spoiling of children in the village school. 'May we ask, dear visitors, to be sparing with the pastry, which is liable to give our little friends indigestion?' Do not feed the animals.

The racism exemplified above came naturally to Britons secure in imperial attitudes, and was evident even in the language of those who disapproved: 'It may be questioned if the exhibition of these poor black creatures is either becoming or edifying.' There were strenuous objections from those who felt Glasgow's purist tradition in exhibitions demeaned by the spectacle: 'It is what one might look for in a tenth-rate waxwork show or a dime museum, but it is altogether unworthy and beneath the dignity of those responsible for the Scottish National Exhibition.'[11] This comment however accurately identified the enormous popular appeal of the two villages.

An Clachan, a Highland Village on the banks of the Caol Abhain, was another very popular attraction. It was on the face of it complementary to the Auld Toon; but located again in the amusement section, charging an admission fee, its appeal was not unlike that of the native encampments described above. Scotland's own 'aborigines' were displayed as an endangered species in their primitive cottages, in picturesque costume, speaking and singing in their strange tongue, and practising their native crafts.

145 and 146 (*opposite*). The West African Village adjacent to the Laplanders, with assembled inhabitants. On the left is the Hall of Festivities where 'performances' of various rituals were staged. Below, a postcard showing 'Wee West Africans' and amused spectators.

147. A photogenic Scottish native in the Highland Village.

On its three-acre site the Clachan was run as a self-contained enterprise, opened on 20 May by the Earl and Countess of Cassillis. All employees were Gaelic-speaking Highlanders. Its commercial purpose was
apparent but of a worthy nature: it was conceived with the 'patriotic object
of arousing a greater interest in the Highland people, in their traditions
and customs, in their beautiful Gaelic language, literature and music, in
their distinctive Celtic art, and especially to afford a unique opportunity
for exhibiting and disposing of Highland Home Industries to the vast
concourse of people who will visit the Exhibition from many lands'. Surplus profits were destined for the Co-operative Council of Highland
Home Industries. With salesgirls decorative in the *Earasaid* or *Arisaid*
worn by 'Highland ladies' of about two hundred years ago and provided
by the Marchioness of Bute, the Village Store turned over a large quantity
of tweeds, plaids, basketwork and other craft products. At the Inn, An
Tigh Osda, lassies in home-spun and tartan served what passed for auth-

148. Assorted inhabitants and visitors among
primitive cottages (their walls made of painted
plaster) in the Highland Village, An Clachan.
The Glasgow buildings behind were brushed
out for album and postcard use of this
photograph.

entic Highland fare, with tea and non-alcoholic heather ale to wash it down: while *uisge beatha* or *usquebagh* was not on the menu, an illicit still could be examined on the outskirts of the village. The other main building, the Big Hoose, was designed internally as a Hall accommodating 350 for Gaelic and Scottish entertainments. A white-washed Kirk was a strictly undenominational 'Village Sanctuary', and other 'typical' structures included a pre-Reformation 'cill' and a chambered cairn.

Some of the huddled cottages were modelled on primitive Highland 'black houses', with peat fires smoking in the middle of earthen floors, others on crofters' homes of the 'but-an'-ben' type. What attracted more attention than their crude simplicity was the amazing realism of painted canvas and plaster stone-walling. To the human interest of representative spinners, pipers, blacksmiths and others going about their daily tasks was added an assortment of animals: a cow for the crofters' Dairy, a Highland pony, a St Kilda sheep, a pair of ravens and an unfortunate wildcat - there was some correspondence in the papers about the caging of such an animal.

In 1911 the organisers of the Exhibition had hit effectively on the essential appeal of such an event. 'Undoubtedly the strongest magnet which an Exhibition has to offer is the opportunity of sitting in the sun and listening to light music, with the accompaniment of light refreshments. That this method of spending leisure hours is foreign to our national genius and frowned on by our climate makes it all the more enjoyable when the opportunity offers itself.' Continuing its reflections the *Glasgow Herald* found the explanation of success 'in the agreeable spectacle of a group of middle-aged, earnest-minded and ordinarily douce business men sitting solemnly back to back on a Joy Wheel'. Almost as soon as it opened there was loud complaint that 10 o'clock was too early to close 'the giddy "X"'.

Visitors this memorable summer to the '"Mecca" of Holiday makers' included Princess Louise, Duchess of Argyll (the daughter of Queen

149. Salesgirls from the Village Store wearing the picturesque Arisaid. All employees of the Clachan were Gaelic-speaking Highlanders.

150. Crowded trams and late-night jollity were a feature of this Exhibition, as of its predecessors. The tower of the Palace of Industry stands out illuminated: the University is soberly silhouetted in the distance. (A postcard.)

THE LAST CAR FROM THE EXHIBITION.

Victoria), and Lord Kitchener. Among foreigners were a June 'Pilgrimage' of American Scots (including 100 from Pittsburgh alone), and a party of New Zealanders in Glasgow to witness the launch of a new armoured cruiser by Fairfield. In July there was what amounted to a 'special exhibit' of 650 Japanese sailors from two of Admiral Togo's warships. In return for making a display of themselves they were treated to a ride on the scenic railway and tea in McKillop's 'popular' restaurant. The evening was always a gay time at the Exhibition (admission was reduced to 6d) and crowds increased still more when the illuminations on the buildings were inaugurated on 11 August. Over 40,000 lights of red and green and white created a night-time fairyland, though the Palace of History remained properly in sober darkness.

The weather was some of the best in living memory. Only twelve 'unfavourable' days were recognised, one of which was the opening. The close too was wet. Rain turned the courts and avenues to mud and stained the buildings: it was easier in such conditions to bid farewell to the year's gaiety. On the closing night, 4 November, a violent storm began the dismantling operation prematurely. Damage to the wall of the Palace of

151. Magnificent panoramic view of the site, taken from the Kelvingrove Art Gallery and Museum (which lay outside the boundaries on this occasion). Right, the Palace of Industry, centre the Palace of History and the Concert Hall beyond. On the left-hand side, beneath Park Terrace, the High Walk leading up to the twin towers of the Aviation Pavilion by the flagstaff, with the dominating curve of the Garden Club below and the curious structures of the amusement area to the left. In the foreground the Auld Toon and Popular Restaurant. All the buildings were temporary.

History laid bare the old building beneath, which fortunately protected the precious exhibits. More spectacularly the roof of the exposed Aviation Pavilion flew into Park Terrace, and the Africans nearby lost their enclosing palisade. Part of the Palace of Industry roof blew off too, but by an extraordinary stroke of good luck for the Exhibition's funds, the building had apparently at midnight become the property of the Motor Trade Association.

Attendances, which had been regularly compared with 1901's, reached by the close 9,369,375, a figure, it was stressed, which did *not* include the large number of attendants - averaging around 7,500 a day in 1901 - which had been deceptively allowed to boost previous totals. The Exhibition had been open for 160 days, as opposed to 165 in 1901. With due allowances therefore it is clear that Glasgow's Scottish Exhibition ran very close to 1901 in attendances, and was a fair match for its splendid International predecessors. Like them it ended in profit. £15,000 was set aside to endow the Chair; £4000 went to the Corporation for restoration of the Park; and the surplus for the vague but honourable purpose of promoting Scottish Art, Literature and Industry.

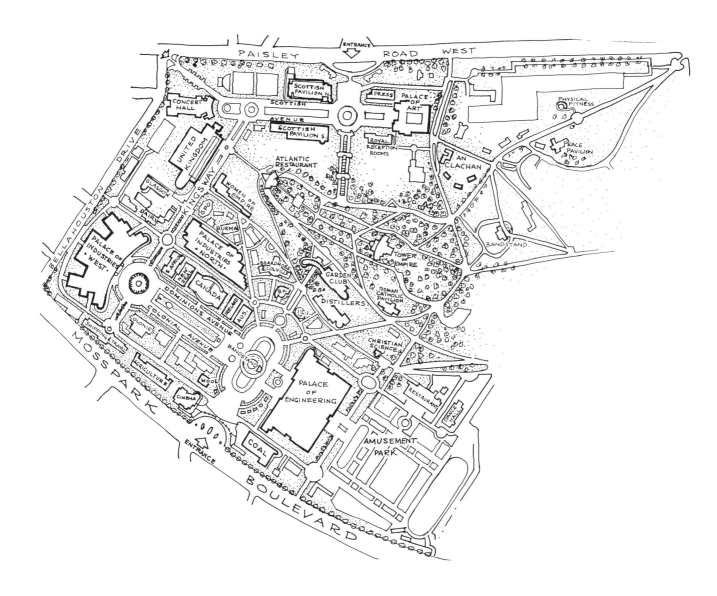

152. The Empire Exhibition (Scotland), 1938, held in Bellahouston Park. (Based on the official plan.)

1938

In the late 1930s Britain was struggling out of deep economic crisis towards the second World War of the century. This was a bold but equally an ideal time to stage the most elaborate and extravagant exhibition ever held in the United Kingdom, or anywhere in the British Empire.

That it should be held in Glasgow was altogether appropriate. As the fiftieth anniversary of its first International Exhibition came round, the Second City of Empire and Scotland as a whole were lagging behind in industrial recovery. Glasgow's specialised economy, dependent on heavy industry and foreign markets, had suffered devastating collapse in the years of depression which followed the brief boom induced by the First

153. Youth and health were idealised throughout the Exhibition, in natural reaction to the recent depression. Here photo-montage and sculpture in the Scottish Pavilion South strike a distinctively 'Thirties' note.

Notes to this chapter appear on page 190.

World War. Notable attempts at diversification had foundered: Beardmore's, the giant of Scotland's metal-founding industry, had invested with characteristic enterprise in the air and automobile industries in an attempt to forge links between old and new, but had retrenched to a heavy industrial base by the early 1930s. The aero-engine and aircraft industry in Scotland, lacking government support, had more or less died out in the late 1920s. Of the four major manufacturers and various smaller firms who were producing cars and commercial vehicles after the First World War, only the Albion Motor Company remained by 1930. But it was the old pride of the Clyde that had suffered the most conspicuous and demoralising decline: by 1934 permanent job losses in shipbuilding and the steel-making and mining industries linked to it had risen to 60,000.

Belatedly and grudgingly Westminster accepted some measure of responsibility for the plight of this once self-sufficient city. A well-aimed gesture was the subsidy in 1933 which enabled work to begin again on the great hulk No. 534, which had been looming in a state of frozen incompleteness over the Clyde's desolate dockyards since 1931. She was launched as the *Queen Mary* in 1934. As the decade drew on public money was injected for a less altruistic purpose. Rearmament, once again the false salvation of Glasgow's heavy industry, brought renewed activity to the shipyards and engineering works, and a new mood of optimism in some quarters. A number of other political initiatives to promote Scottish industry were taken. In 1934 the Secretary of State for Scotland appointed a Commissioner for Special Areas, and there followed the launch of the Industrial Estates Company and the Scottish Special Areas Housing Association. But more flamboyant was the proposal for a huge Exhibition. In June 1936 the Finance and General Purposes Committee of the Scottish National Development Council was created to plan it, largely at the prompting of Sir James Lithgow and other leaders of business and industry.

At the inaugural meeting on 5 October 1936, the motion that the Exhibition be held was proposed by the Lord Provost of Edinburgh. This diplomatic move acknowledged the traditional antagonism between the two cities and was an attempt to avert the inevitable indignation in Edinburgh about the location of the event. But Glasgow's status as Second City of Empire was unchallenged and its merits as a venue for an Exhibition of Empire were indisputable. On the one hand the city was the focus for Scotland's industrial decline and had some of the worst living conditions, overcrowding and unemployment in Europe. But despite severe economic battering it remained a major world manufacturing and mercantile centre and the premier port in Scotland. It was very accessible, with half the Scottish population living within a 25-mile radius of the city. Glasgow's record in staging major and successful exhibitions was also strongly in its favour.

Against the background of a stagnating economy and inner city squalor the Exhibition came as an extraordinary expression of hope for the future - a hope cruelly annulled by the events which followed so soon upon it. The ideals upon which the Exhibition was founded were high. The *Official Guide* stated its five Objects:

1. To illustate the progress of the British Empire at home and overseas.

2. To show the resources and the potentialities of the United Kingdom and the Empire Overseas to the new generations.

3. To stimulate Scottish work and production and to direct attention to Scotland's historical and scenic attractions.

4. To foster Empire trade and a closer friendship among the peoples of the British Commonwealth of Nations.

5. To emphasise to the world the peaceful aspirations of the peoples of the British Empire.

The commitment here to progress and education, and the aim of boosting regional industry, commerce and tourism repeat elements familiar from Glasgow's earlier Exhibitions. Objects 4 and 5 however reflect clearly the troubled times in which this great show took place. The threat of war was also tacitly acknowledged in Neville Chamberlain's Prime Ministerial introductory message: 'Now, perhaps more than at any other time, there is a need for mutual understanding and co-operation between the nations.' When the Exhibition was complete the shadow of war was visible in the façade murals of the Palace of Engineering which featured warships and planes. There was an overt display of rearmament in the Services Pavilion, which advertised the Army and Royal Air Force, and in the Navy kiosk nearby. The hope of peace was represented in the small wooden Peace Pavilion (designed by Alister MacDonald, son of the late Prime Minister) and a Peace Cairn in the backwoods of the Exhibition.

154. The Peace Pavilion, with its carillon and bucolic figures, reflected contemporary anxiety about developments in Europe.

With tension growing in Europe a parade of Empire offered a comforting show of strength. The claim that this unity was founded on friendship attempted to disguise the disintegration of the old imperial certainties.

The restriction of the Exhibition to 'Empire' (like Britain's last big exhibition, at Wembley in 1924-5), was disagreeable to vocal members of the Independent Labour Party on the Glasgow City Council. As International Socialists they would have preferred a broader, and in the circumstances clearly unrealistic, assertion of international brotherhood; but international status was anyway forbidden by the Convention signed in 1928 governing the frequency of universal exhibitions. On the question of finance the ILP was again thwarted when it urged that the Corporation fund the Exhibition. They wanted the City to be the beneficiary of the considerable profit that was envisaged. All the previous Glasgow Exhibitions had been good money spinners. The bad experience of Wembley, which despite being extended for a second season ended in substantial deficit, was overlooked. An English exhibition would never be considered a standard of comparison by patriots who still saw Scottish affairs as a separate entity.

In the end the Exhibition was funded much as its predecessors had been, from a guarantee fund which within the first six months of its existence raised £750,000, half as much again as the original cost estimate. Donors included the Glasgow Corporation, other local authorities, the Scottish banks, major industrial concerns, small businesses and individuals. Amounts ranged from £40,000, the joint contribution from the banks, to £2 from individuals: confident in Glasgow's tradition of success in this field few doubted that their money was safe. Additional funding from central government, which paid for the UK Pavilion and contributed £20,000 to the Scottish buildings, and from the Dominions, Colonies and companies who paid for their own pavilions and displays resulted in a total estimated cost of around £10 million, a vast sum. While the Exhibition was designed to emphasise the higher aspirations of the British Empire and overt commercial interests were played down, a profit would have embarrassed no one. For individual exhibitors the retailing and advertising arrangements within the Exhibition seem to have been very open, with few restrictions on sales from palaces, pavilions and kiosks in the grounds.

In addition to inaugurating the fund-raising campaign the October 1936 meeting had also confirmed the site for the Exhibition. This was to be Bellahouston Park in the depressed south west area of the city, selected because of the size of the proposed event. Kelvingrove Park, more prestigious and more accessible from the centre of Glasgow, had seen all three previous major exhibitions, but lacked sufficient level terrain to accommodate the enormous event now planned. Despite the hill rising to 150 ft in the centre of the Park, Bellahouston offered around 150 acres of level ground. In addition Bellahouston had the advantage of being an island site, bounded on two sides by major roads, Paisley Road West to the north and Mosspark Boulevard to the south. As far as the planning of Glasgow's exhibitions was concerned the motor car was a new phenomenon, though

155. The red Scottish, and imperial, lion, the Exhibition's logo.

EMPIRE EXHIBITION SCOTLAND 1938

156. Thomas S. Tait (circled in the middle) and his team of architects. From top left: T. W. Marwick, Margaret Brodie, Launcelot Ross, Esme Gordon, Gordon Tait, Jack Coia, J. Taylor Thomson, A. D. Bryce and Basil Spence. (*Scottish Architect and Builder's Journal*)

its ownership did not reach below the middle class: the site was easily reached by car and 10,000 parking places were provided. Furthermore the park was virgin territory without the existing roads, pathways and features which had hindered grand architectural layouts at Kelvingrove. This allowed complete freedom in the planning of the Exhibition.

The task of creating an Exhibition of international scale and quality required a designer of extraordinary ability. With just over eighteen months in hand from sketch plan to completion the labour of co-ordinating work on site was immense. Although design competitions were in vogue and had been used for many prestigious projects, the planning committee considered that the procedure, though desirable, was not practical. Instead their unanimous choice for the job of Architect-in-Chief was Thomas Smith Tait of the London firm of Sir John Burnet, Tait and

Lorne. Tait, born in Paisley and educated in Glasgow, had recently completed the important government commission for St Andrew's House, Calton Hill, Edinburgh. Burnet, senior partner of the firm, was the most highly respected living Scottish architect. Tait was 'recognised on all hands as being the right man for this job', and had agreed to work with 'one or two of the younger school of Scottish architects'.[1] According to

Esme Gordon, an architect who worked in Tait's office during the 1930s, his boss was a very practical man and a confirmed workaholic.

The Exhibition's complex rôle, to illustrate the British Empire and demonstrate the United Kingdom's, and specifically Scotland's, own progress and resources, required three main categories of building. Tait aimed to group together in distinct areas the pavilions of Dominions and Colonies, buildings representing the life and culture of the British Isles, and buildings which demonstrated British achievement in engineering and manufacturing. The Architect-in-Chief revelled in his task and the thrill of being able to say 'Let there be an avenue here and here and here'. Faced with a planning problem of this nature Tait favoured using a scale contour model of the site on which were arranged and rearranged wooden blocks representing each of the buildings, and this method was almost certainly used for the layout of the Empire Exhibition.

Tait presented his ground plan in February 1937. Its arrangement was essentially simple. The two biggest buildings, the Palace of Engineering and the Palace of Industry, were located on the largest plots available, to the south of the central hill, at either end of the Dominions and Colonial

157. An early model of the site, looking north, showing the location of the major buildings. The Palace of Industry envisaged at this stage was not big enough and a second (clearly visible in the photograph opposite) was built over the site occupied in this model by the Palace of Fashion, which became the Women of Empire Pavilion.

158. Bird's-eye view of what was built, looking south east, with the Palace of Engineering top right and the Garden Club (a more soberly named version of what appears as the 'Lucullus Restaurant' in the model opposite) top left. Below the Garden Club are some substantial company buildings. The South African pavilion at the bottom of the picture stands out distinctly from the modernity of the rest.

Avenues. These industrial buildings were to be separated from pavilions representing the nations of Empire by large and elaborately planted flowerbeds. The two rows of buildings representing the Dominions and the Colonies respectively were divided by a long narrow pond. This was designed to give the visitor the impression of two separate avenues. To the west of the hill, at right angles to the Dominions and Colonial Avenues, ran the avenue later named 'Kingsway' upon which the United Kingdom Pavilion was sited. On the north side of the hill ran the Scottish Avenue, flanked by two mirror-image Scottish Pavilions, and closed at either end by buildings devoted to culture, the Concert Hall and Palace of Art.

Although most of the important structures were built upon the three avenues, the dramatic potential of the hill was acknowledged in Tait's submission. The City Parks Department had insisted on the preservation of the existing 'amenity' of the site. This, roughly translated, meant that they wanted to keep all the mature trees. The area on the top of the hill was therefore severely restricted for building purposes. The solution was to build high. Along with his layout plan Tait presented sketches for an observation tower to be built on the summit of the hill. Two massive stairways in a direct line with the two Exhibition entrances would give easy access to it. The area to the east of the Park was not regarded as part of the Exhibition proper and was not part of Tait's design remit. Instead it was designated for an amusement park and, in recognition of the popularity of the Clachan at the 1911 Exhibition, a reconstruction of a Highland Village.

As far as architectural style was concerned the tight timescale ruled out elaborate or highly detailed buildings. Arming himself for a complete break with the historical dress commonly associated with exhibition architecture, Tait declared that an essentially modern style was vital for this forward-looking Exhibition: 'We cannot try to erect buildings in the old, mediaeval style of architecture where there are certain structural features which necessitate modern treatment and modern requirements with big spacing which the old mediaeval architecture would not allow us to carry out.'[2] The sweeping (and inaccurate) dismissal of what had gone before as 'the old mediaeval style' may have overstressed the point, but Tait was well used to the conservatism of the British public and their antipathy to the style which the French referred to as 'Nudisme'.

Tait also emphasised that the buildings were intended to combine dignity and gaiety: 'Dignity because the whole empire was taking part; gaiety because when John Citizen goes to an exhibition he considers himself on holiday and wants to escape from everyday things.' He goes on to describe the 'long clean lines' and unified colour scheme of the Exhibition. Then, sounding rather like the architectural guru Le Corbusier, he explains the adoption of a construction technique using steel frames and cladding materials. Similar methods had been used in Glasgow's Exhibitions of 1901 and 1911, but to produce deceptive pastiches of permanent structures. Here Tait gives an eloquent exposition of his views on the relationship between form and function in architecture.

Good building and good architecture are simply the honest use of the materials you have to handle. A concrete building should be as different from one made of brick as an oil painting is different from a watercolour. Consequently, when an architect has suddenly to switch over from building in a permanent way with stone and steel to temporary structures of light steel, wood and asbestos, he has to reorganise his ideas. If he simply imitates permanent architecture, he will create something as ridiculous as a Greek temple of reinforced concrete. Big temporary buildings mean a new technique.

The buildings at Bellahouston are, therefore, ones which are suited to the function they have to fulfill and the materials from which they are made. They are long and low, because light steelwork lends itself to big spans. They have great sweeping lines, partly because steelwork is suited to the purpose and partly to take advantage of the effect and dignity and lightness which can be so obtained. And they have been easily erected and will be as easily dismantled. Some people may call them modernist. That is a word I do not like. In this case it means nothing, for the design has been conditioned by function and materials, and not by time.[3]

The Exhibition's buildings were constructed using both steel and timber frames. The cladding material to suit both was asbestos-cement sheet-

159. Every detail was carefully designed, down to the unobtrusive green litter-bins. They were more noticeable once liberally plastered with advertising posters.

160. Work progressing on the site, showing clearly the steel frame construction of the buildings. The skeleton of Tait's Tower, built without scaffolding, dominates the scene. The South Cascade and stairway is laid out on the left and the decorative pillars of the ICI Pavilion are well advanced.

161. The tower and vane motif appeared throughout the Exhibition, as here in the pair of matching Scottish Pavilions, and the North Cascade down Bellahouston Hill. The picture also captures the contrast between the bright new temporary buildings and their blackened urban setting.

ing, which was available in large quantities, was light, easy to handle, stood up well to all weather conditions and was easy to paint. By using standard materials Tait gave the Exhibition order and unity. Buildings which were the work of many architects blended in their modernity, their scale, materials and use of a limited range of harmonious colours. In addition Tait determined that the design of kiosks, lamp standards and litter bins would conform to that of the larger structures and contribute to the unity of the overall scheme. The admirable consistency of the finished scheme was attributed to the fact that 'every detail was either under the direct invention of Tait's pencil, or in some degree under his personal control'.[4]

At the peak of its construction the Empire Exhibition employed over 3000 men, which brought an immediate injection of life into the building industry. When complete it was the size of a small town, and the most concentrated and comprehensive display of the 'New Architecture' seen anywhere in Britain before the War of 1939-45. *Scottish Field* (without doubt the main oracle of the Scottish middle classes) was effusive: 'The meadows of England have their own blossom in May: this one year we need not envy them, for a miracle has flowered in a Glasgow suburb. These aren't the kind of flowers we are accustomed to. The Palaces at the Exhibition are very different from any of our three main styles of architecture - the Baronial, the Classical and the Mock-turtle. Their lines show them to be clean and seemly and spacious (three most admirable qualities in any sort of house), and they are the proper expressions of an efficient age, while Tait's tower rises out of them like efficiency enchanted by imagination.'[5]

The unrestrained praise in the press fired public enthusiasm for the event. Despite the scale of the Exhibition and the short building time (a mere fourteen months), Tait's system enabled it to break all records, and unlike the Paris Exhibition a year earlier Glasgow's was ready in time. On 3 May 1938, as Hitler met Mussolini in Rome, the gates opened to admit 150,000 visitors. In his opening address at the nearby Ibrox Stadium (used in conjunction with the Exhibition for such mass events), King George VI declared the Empire Exhibition a 'symbol of the vitality and initiative upon which the continued prosperity of Scotland must rest'. Lord Elgin, President of the Exhibition, replied with stirring confidence: 'Scotland is proud to have the privilege of staging this symbol of unity of the British people. In Bellahouston Park, Glasgow, there have been gathered together exhibits illustrating the resources of the whole British Empire, resources which are limitless, which are produced and directed by a people whose capacity for work is also limitless, whose capacity for play at the proper time is boundless, and whose desire is for peace.'

Their Majesties then moved into the Exhibition to enjoy this display of limitless resources in the United Kingdom Pavilion, the Burma Pavilion, the Canadian Pavilion (where Her Majesty purchased two Shirley Temple dolls for the little princesses, who had to wait to a later date for their visit to the Exhibition), the Scottish Pavilions and the Palace of Engineering. The King and Queen lunched in the Atlantic restaurant, the most luxurious of the Exhibition's public eating places, which commanded views over the western end of the site. Royal Reception Rooms had been provided for their use next to the Palace of Art. Like the comparable suites at Glasgow's 1888 and 1901 Exhibitions, these lavish apartments had been furnished and decorated by the firm of Wylie and Lochhead, working in collaboration with Tait. Quantities of Nigerian pear wood and Glamis fabric were used in the scheme. Soft turquoise blue was the predominant colour in the main rooms, but the bathroom suite was magnificently primrose.[6] The facilities were well used throughout the six months' run of the Exhibition by visiting Royals and VIPs.

162 (*opposite*). King George VI and Queen Elizabeth on opening day, leaving the United Kingdom Pavilion by its monumental exit.

163. The central bandstand, and behind it the pavilions of ICI and Distillers, and the Garden Club, all beneath the Tower. The Roman Catholic Pavilion stands on the hill to the right.

Sited in strategic proximity to the Reception Rooms, facing them across the 'Arts Court' in fact, was the Press Club, where representatives of the nation's papers eagerly processed news of what important people were doing, saying or wearing. According to the *Bulletin*, on opening day Queen Elizabeth, who was beautifully dressed in harmonising tones of pale grey, was particularly delighted by her visit to the Women's Pavilion. 'Her real interest and knowledge of domestic matters caused great satisfaction among those who were busily making scones or laying out tempting and dietetically correct meals in the gleaming domestic section.' The monarchy's growing skill in public relations is amply attested in accounts of this and other royal visits to the Empire Exhibition. Two other highlights of Their Majesties' day which appealed to the press were the inevitable trip up the Tower, and a visit to the Highland Clachan where Mary Morrison from Barra sang them a lament while working at her spinning wheel outside the Lewis cottage. Queen Mary was among other dignitaries to be treated later to this spectacle, and listened intently to Mrs Morrison's rendering, in Gaelic, of 'Leaving Barra'.

The royal visitors' experience of the Exhibition was predictably far from typical. One day's visit could not hope to be exhaustive, and the route chosen for the King and Queen was more select than most, taking in the most important buildings and those where omission would have caused the greatest offence. 'John Citizen' would do things differently. He might arrive on a tram, perhaps on the circular route specially laid on for

164. The Palace of Engineering with its belli-
cose murals. The construction of warships and
armaments had revived Glasgow's declining
heavy industry.

the Exhibition. His journey from St Vincent Street would take him past
the Paisley Road West entrance which offered one possible starting point
for his tour. If he stayed on board he would catch tempting glimpses as he
circled the site of the Scottish Pavilions, the Concert Hall, the Atlantic
restaurant built like the prow of a ship on the brow of Bellahouston Hill,
the backs of the United Kingdom Pavilion and the Palace of Industry
West, and, rising above all, Tait's Tower. Alighting at the main entrance
on Mosspark Boulevard, he would pay his shilling, and sixpence for his
children, just as his grandfather had done fifty years before. Once past the
turnstile our visitor might set off towards the colonnaded entrance of the
Palace of Engineering.

Built in only three months this was by far the largest of the Exhibition's
buildings, covering five acres. Its sheer scale recalled the great Machinery
Halls of Glasgow's 1888 and 1901 International Exhibitions, and underlined the continued significance to the Scottish economy of heavy industry, and the urgent need to promote it. In addition several major firms
occupied their own pavilions, and there were separate buildings for Coal
and Shipping. The Palace housed many technical exhibits and demonstrations of various processes, as well as domestic appliances, and models of
dams, bridges and ships. The layman's eye would be caught by an illuminated revolving globe of the world, said to be the largest ever constructed. On a similar superlative scale a full-size model of Britain's largest
steel ingot (230 tons) was shown entering a fiery furnace.

165. Looking towards the Dominions Avenue and the pavilions of Canada, New Zealand and South Africa, with the Palace of Industries West at the far end.

Bypassing the central bandstand and heading for the Dominions Avenue the visitor would come first to the Australian Pavilion with its two distinctive vertical red fins. Here all varieties of fleece in their natural state, straight from the sheep, were shown, along with displays of minerals and wine, and a grocer's shop selling typical dairy and farm produce. Real song-birds chirruped in a cage-bound Australian bush scene, and a model of Sidney Harbour Bridge (whose piers had been designed by Thomas Tait) sat in a pool with ferries passing under and cars and trains over it. The Pavilion of Independent Ireland next door might have been thought a little too close to home to be a huge draw, but it appealed to Glasgow's large immigrant Irish population.

Maintaining a strong tradition of exhibiting at Glasgow's Exhibitions, the huge Canadian Pavilion was centrally located on the Dominions Avenue. This was the largest non-United Kingdom Pavilion, and its scale and cultural content emphasised the long-established autonomy of the Canadian people. The film 'Rose Marie', released in 1936, where the Mountie (Nelson Eddy) got his man and the girl (Janette MacDonald), had conjured up a romantic image of Canada which was exploited to the full. There were four mounted policemen in attendance at all times, and they would, on request, sign souvenir brochures for swooning admirers.

166. Looking towards the Colonial Avenue, and the Palace of Industries West. Submarine floodlights of changing colour illuminated the spectacular water displays when darkness fell.

The Canadian Pavilion was virtually windowless, relying on interior lighting effects to illuminate the educational displays which were characteristic of this Exhibition. Dioramas and paintings showed aspects of Canadian life not easily exhibited - important buildings, industry, sport and education. Beside the entrance a giant mural, 14 ft high and 46 ft long, depicted the life and culture of the nation. A 600 sq ft burnished copper illuminated map showed Canadian forestry, mining, aerodromes and universities. The building also served as a shop-window for thirty Canadian firms whose displays included electrical machinery, canned goods, dairy and other food produce. The Canadian National Parks Bureau, arguably more sympathetic to wildlife than their Australian counterparts, displayed stuffed exhibits showing the wide variety of wildlife in the Canadian peaks. More dead animals were on show in the form of pelts.

Like the other dominions the New Zealand Pavilion next door to Canada displayed meat, dairy produce, canned food, pelts, timber and minerals, demonstrating the crucial importance of the Empire's resources, especially food, to a far from self-sufficient mother country. The pavilion also featured photographs of Maoris, who were idealistically claimed to be 'equal partners in New Zealand, enjoying the same rights of citizenship and opportunity, sharing the same benefits of education and social ser-

167. The Australian Pavilion.

168. The New Zealand Pavilion.

vices, united in devotion to the Empire and loyalty to the British Throne'. The arms emblazoned above the entrance gave aborigine and white man equal status.

The native population of South Africa was not a picturesque minority: the *Official Guide* refers only to fifteen busts of 'typical' members of native tribes, and the work of Bantu craftsmen shown 'side by side with sculpture and painting by modern South African artists'. The South African Pavilion was remarkable for its complete lack of sympathy with the architectural 'modernism' of the rest of the Exhibition. It was built in the Dutch colonial style which represented a national architecture, though the Afrikaaners were not politically dominant at this period. That this design was by the long-established Glasgow practice of James Miller, architect of

169. View down Kingsway, with the South African Pavilion in the foreground. Beyond are the Palace of Industries North and the GPO building.

170. The Pavilion of Southern Rhodesia, advertising one of the Exhibition's principal sights, with the Empire Tea Pavilion beyond.

the 1901 Exhibition and still practising at the age of 78, is intriguing. Over the intervening years his firm's output had been very varied. Why Tait allowed this disruptive design is not known, but respect for Miller was perhaps a factor. Tait's fears of public antipathy to the Exhibition's prevailing style were more than justified by the enthusiastic reaction to this backward-looking structure. *The Glasgow Herald* reported the popular feeling that this of all the buildings on the site should be retained. 'With its white walls, brown roof, solid wooden doors and stepped gable this pavilion stands out among the utilitarian architecture of the other buildings in the park and most visitors to the Exhibition have been impressed by its design.' As J. M. Richards observed, South Africa had produced something 'entirely unsuitable' but 'must be excused for doing it well'.[7]

Crossing from the South African pavilion the visitor would certainly pause to gaze at what were claimed as the most spectacular water displays ever mounted for any exhibition. The formal lake between the Dominions and Colonial Avenues featured two flare fountains flanked by eighteen subsidiary fountains. This was all dramatic enough during the day but took on quite a different aspect by night, when phased floodlighting changed the colour of the fountains in a cycle of red, blue, green and yellow. Coloured lighting also illuminated the cascades which ran down the north and south sides of the hill.

For the indefatigable visitor determined to see the whole Exhibition the western end of the lake signalled a return journey down the Colonial Avenue to the bandstand. On this side were represented some of the Empire's more colourful subjects. The Composite Colonial Pavilion contained the natural treasures of Malaya, the West Indies, Cyprus, Malta, Ceylon, North Borneo, the Falkland Islands, Somaliland, Bechuanaland, St Helena and Hong Kong. In the central hall a tropical scene with rubber and mango trees, tea and coffee bushes, rice and maize, was combined with an industrial display and a shore scene to represent all the products and exports of these countries. Elsewhere there were exhibits like Malaya's display of the pineapple industry, with full-size models of Chinese cutters and canners, and demonstrations of cooking with pineapples. The arts and crafts of Colonial natives were displayed, but no use seems to have been made of the live artisans who were so popular at the earlier Exhibitions.

171 (*opposite*). The numerous fountains of the Exhibition made a deep impression on visitors accustomed to urban grime.

172. The Burma Pavilion, sited away from the Colonial Avenue, next to the Chiver's building. Here native exuberance overcame the general exclusion of applied decoration in the Exhibition's architectural style.

The importance of tea to the people of the British Empire, and in particular to the home population, was apparent from the pavilion wholly devoted to it, housing displays of tea production and a collection of historic tea pots. This was essentially a marketing exercise by the Empire Tea Market Expansion Bureau, working on behalf of India, Ceylon and the Dutch East Indies (which had slipped in from another empire on false pretences). This was surprisingly the only representation of India, a restive member of the Empire, though the amusement park featured an Indian Theatre.

Next to the Empire Tea Pavilion sat the combined exhibit of Southern Rhodesia and East Africa. Like others on the Colonial Avenue this pavilion had a nondescript exterior, but within was a spectacle which put it third in the Exhibiton's popularity stakes (after the Clachan and the Tower). A reconstruction of 'the greatest river wonder of the world', the Victoria Falls, 120 ft wide and 14 ft deep, cascaded at a rate of more than one and a half million gallons per day. Coloured lights changed the scene from dawn to night on a five minute cycle, and a model train travelled across a bridge below the falls. The roar of the river was reproduced by loudspeakers, while lights played on steam to make rainbows. After this drama a visit to more conventional displays of cattle-cake and postage stamps in the West African Colonies Pavilion must have been something of an anticlimax. However the quality of the section devoted to Nigeria was impressive. The Nigerian government had sought the best available and, like other wealthy exhibitors, employed the services of Thomas Tait to design its display.

The narrow avenue behind the Colonial Avenue was dominated by an eye-catching Jacob's ram atop the Wool Pavilion. This stood on its ped-

173. The RAC was canvassing for members beneath the Wool Pavilion.

174 (*opposite*). The curved front of the Palace of Industries West, its gigantic mural decoration, like much of the Exhibition's imagery, giving an ideal balance between male and female. Stormy skies made for dramatic photographs but were unfortunately characteristic of the dreadful summer weather.

estal opposite the Empire Cinema, which was run by the eminent historian of Glasgow, Charles Oakley. The scale of the building, for a city with a movie obsession (Glasgow had a greater ratio of cinemas to population than anywhere other than New York), was very modest. Daily showings of Charlie Chaplin and historic footage of events like Queen Victoria's funeral ensured a popularity in proportion to the size of the building.

Doubling back on the south side of the avenue, the visitor found next to the Cinema the resources of the British Isles on display in the Agriculture,

Fisheries and Forestry Pavilion. Here, for example, the whole process of bacon production (bar the grisly bits) was given in the Ulster section. Like many of the Exhibition's displays this pavilion sought to educate the public with a number of prosaic exhibits, and its appeal was limited. The Shipping and Travel Pavilion at the western end of this range was rather more adventurous. 'Art' was used here as throughout the Exhibition to project and elevate facets of modern life. With its murals depicting the Spirit of Travel and sculptural allegories of rail and sea transport, its propaganda was neither as overt nor as unpalatable as that of its neighbour.

Leaving the Shipping and Travel Pavilion the visitor found himself once more at the west end of the lake, outside the first industrial building. Like the Palace of Engineering the Palace of Industries West presented a giant front to the end of the Dominions and Colonial Avenues. Here the entrance was a great curve. The three projecting display halls fanning out behind gave the building an E form in plan. Light filtered through the predominantly glazed roof to show exhibits from manufacturing industry in the United Kingdom: cosmetics, chemicals, furniture and fancy goods, musical instruments, office appliances, leisure goods, textiles, printing and stationery, foods and beverages. While there was some emphasis upon Scottish firms local concerns did not dominate as they had at Glasgow's earlier Exhibitions. There had been no exhibition on a comparable scale in Britain since Wembley in 1924-5, and everyone was keen to grasp the

opportunity it offered. Early demand on the far from limited space required the construction of a second building. This, the Palace of Industries North, was erected at great speed on a site extending along behind the Dominions Avenue, with a narrow frontage to Kingsway.

The building, entered through a glazed drum, was designed by the young Glasgow architect J. A. Coia. Coia's experience was largely on commissions for the Roman Catholic Church in Glasgow, and he had produced a number of fine brick buildings with Romanesque and Gothic echoes. In construction and style this was a complete break. The timetable

for construction of the rest of the Exhibition was tight, but with the Palace of Industries North Tait's system was tested to the limit. Armed with sketches from the master, Coia set to and produced what was universally regarded as one of the Exhibition's triumphs. There is no doubt that he was helped by a workforce now well accustomed to the clad-frame technique. This design, or at least the parts of it seen by the public, took the 'Exhibition style' to its ultimate - exposing structure, cutting in and out, abutting square sections to the rounded drum, curving the roof (aircraft hangar-like) on the short wing and sticking to the more regular flat and pitched roofing for the bulk of the building. It is ironic that this building, which really summed up what Tait was trying to achieve in the Exhibition's architecture, stood next to the maverick South African Pavilion.

If by this stage of the tour the visitor was in need of refreshment his options were considerable. The grounds were scattered with about twenty restaurants and milk bars, ranging from 'De Luxe' through 'First Class' to 'Popular' (the Garden Club was too exclusive to feature in the *Guide's* listing). Closest to Coia's Industry building, indeed annexed to it, was the Milanda Café, graded 'Popular' and seating 100. Right opposite were a milk bar attached to the Scottish Milk Marketing Board's Model Dairy (which was complete with cows), and Ross's Dairy and Snack Bar.

The only no-smoking restaurant on site was in the Women of Empire Pavilion a little further up Kingsway. The Countess of Elgin and Kin-

175. The Palace of Industries North, approached by a party of the school children who were frequent visitors to the site. Its glazed drum was a recurring feature of the Exhibition's architectural style.

176 (*opposite*). View across the pool outside the United Kingdom Pavilion to the Women of Empire Pavilion, and the Atlantic restaurant, shaped whimsically like the bow of a ship, on Bellahouston Hill above.

177 (*opposite*). Margaret Brodie's design for the Women of Empire Pavilion. (*Official Guide*)

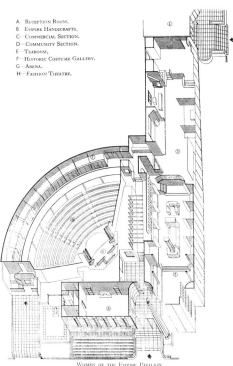

A RECEPTION ROOM.
B EMPIRE HANDICRAFTS.
C COMMERCIAL SECTION.
D—COMMUNITY SECTION.
E—TEAROOM.
F—HISTORIC COSTUME GALLERY.
G—ARENA.
H—FASHION THEATRE.

WOMEN OF THE EMPIRE PAVILION

cardine, convener of the Women's Committee, and wife of the Exhibition's President, saw this building as a haven for the female visitor, its contents designed to entertain and 'enrich the mind'. 'It is one of the most noticeable buildings in the Park, and the architecture without is as commanding as the interior decoration and mural work are fascinating.'[8] The embellishment included a courtyard relief by Norman Forrest depicting 'the rise of woman from bondage to freedom'. Like the rest of the Exhibition the exterior was finished in carefully chosen hues (co-ordinated colouring had hit exhibition architecture with the 1915 San Francisco Exposition). The russet Palace of Industries North and the striking post-office red of the GPO building immediately next door complimented the Women of Empire's dove grey, blue and silver. Its interior was finished in French grey, 'a colour chosen, after consultation, as being kindest to female complexions', according to *Scottish Field*. The pavilion was designed by the brilliant Miss Margaret Brodie, who worked in Tait's office. She was far from being a token woman, and Tait employed her dynamism and resourcefulness to the full. She was site architect for much of the six month lead-in to the Exhibition and was clearly an important influence. On opening day, reported the *Bulletin*, 'the largest picture hat was that of Miss Margaret Brodie A.R.I.B.A., architect of the Pavilion'.

Miss Brodie was of course the exception proving the rule of general male dominance of all important aspects of the Exhibition. Outside the Women of Empire Pavilion women's organisational talents were restricted to a few places on 'appropriate' committees - those for the Garden Club, the Highlands, Horticulture and Hospitality. The Pavilion itself had sections on arts and crafts and welfare work; but reflecting contemporary attitudes, and in contrast to the Women's Industries sections of Glasgow's 1888 and 1901 Exhibitions, the focus was firmly upon woman as homemaker. To some 'in the light of present tendencies there may seem an undue emphasis on the domestic note - but the majority will still agree that home and its interests remain woman's principle concern the world over.'[9] Domestic science was glamourised in a manner that would be revived after the impending war in an effort to get women back into the home. A major attraction of the Pavilion was its 400-seater fashion theatre with a fan-shaped roof covered in muslin folds. Here mannequins paraded the latest British-designed fashions. A History of Fashion exhibition featured over one hundred dresses dating from 1760 to the modern day. The emphasis was on grand dressing and there were a number of costumes with royal connections, including the blue silk gown worn by Queen Victoria at the Great Exhibition in London in 1851. The public's enthusiasm for the previous year's Coronation was reflected in a display of ceremonial robes and reproduction regalia. Ornamental butterflies of Coronation purple or crimson velvet were sold at the exit for charity.

Emerging from the refinement of the Women of Empire Pavilion the visitor was confronted by the white mass of the United Kingdom (sometimes referred to as the British Government) Pavilion. This, the largest of

178 (*left*). Government propaganda exploited modern exhibition techniques in the United Kingdom Pavilion's Fitter Britain Hall: from a postcard.

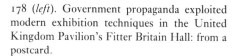

FITTER BRITAIN HALL, UNITED KINGDOM PAVILION, EMPIRE EXHIBITION, SCOTLAND, 1938.

179 (*opposite*) and 180. Fine lions guarded the entrance to the United Kingdom Pavilion.

the national buildings, was by the architect of the Mersey Tunnel, Herbert Rowse. While it lacked the lightness and finesse which Tait had attempted to apply to the Exhibition, it was undoubtedly impressive, and was considered by Sir Cecil M. Weir, Convener of the Exhibition's Council of Management, the finest pavilion by a government at any exhibition. The entrance, flanked by two giant columns, was guarded by stylised British lions. Inside, British achievement was displayed in four halls. The contemporary preoccupation with health and fitness (there was a Physical Fitness Pavilion on the outskirts of the site) was reflected in the Fitter Britain Exhibit. Here an 11 ft high mechanical man represented the operations of the human body in terms of engineering: a camera for the eyes, a pump for the heart and coloured balls jostling through the alimentary canal. The three other halls for Coal, Iron and Steel, and Shipbuilding, concentrated on scientific and industrial research, including coal processing techniques and a model blast furnace. There was also a full scale reproduction of the wheel house of a modern cargo liner. An enormous illuminated globe covered with patches of red proclaimed Britain's continued (but diminishing) authority in the world.

Emerging once more into daylight the visitor would pass on to the Scottish Avenue, noticing the pavilions of those two props of British culture, *The Times* and the BBC, at the junction with Kingsway. At the western extremity he might pause at the Concert Hall. Leading orchestras like the London Symphony Orchestra under Sir Henry Wood, or Sir

Thomas Beecham with the London Philharmonic had been engaged, but the programme was more likely to offer recitals on the Hammond organ and the variety attractions which were a staple of popular entertainment at this period - like Ralphono ('A Fantasy in Smoke'), Donavan and Hayes ('almost acrobats'), or Ivor Moreton and Dave Kaye ('the original Tiger Rag-a-Muffins'). Stars brought to the Exhibition included Will Fyffe, Jack Hylton and Paul Robeson. Band music, so popular at the previous Exhibitions, was still an important feature, with performances from marching bands and regular concerts from the two bandstands, each accommodating 3000 listeners on the Exhibition's ubiquitous green folding chairs.

In contrast to the clutter of the other avenues, the Scottish Avenue only really offered four venues. Two of these were the matching Scottish Pavilions, coloured in shades of patriotic blue. In the North the displays echoed those of the United Kingdom Pavilion, with more propaganda for the public services. The entrance hall was dominated by a statue by Thomas Whalen of *Service*, clutching the Torch of Knowledge in her right hand and the Staff of Health in her left. In a nation where infant and child mortality rates were among the worst in Europe, recent innovations in health care were given understandable prominence, with murals depicting health care from before birth to old age. Also lavishly promoted was Planning, another growing preoccupation, identified with hopes of a better future. The highlight here was a detailed survey of the Aberdeen and District Regional Plan which advocated ideas which must have seemed extraordinary at the time, like densities as low as 12 houses to the acre. The plan was shown on 21 sq ft of glass. A large relief map of Scotland displayed her communications network and the variety of her landscape and resources. In another hall Scottish education was demonstrated by the work of pupils from infant to leaving certificate stages, and a 140 ft long mural showed symbolical representations of educational activities. Outside the North Pavilion five figures set on the wall depicted great Scottish achievers: Robert Burns, Walter Scott, Thomas Carlyle, David Livingstone and James Watt.

The layout of the South Pavilion reflected that of the North. Here the statue in the entrance hall was a giant plaster effigy of the young St Andrew by Archibald Dawson. Dawson, Head of Sculpture at the Glasgow School of Art, was helped to create this 25 ft high monster by his students, who transported plaster to the site in a wheelbarrow and assisted in the physical effort of creating this grand symbol of the power and unity of Scotland. Shortly after completing the statue Dawson died suddenly, so for the duration of the Exhibition it was his memorial. Light shone on the young St Andrew through a more traditional image of the saint bearing the Saltire Cross on which he was martyred, painted on the window behind. This pavilion housed the Scottish historical displays prominent at the previous Exhibitions, with artefacts and depictions covering Scotland's past from Roman times on through the ever popular Mary Queen of Scots and Jacobite relics, finishing with the personal effects of

181 (*opposite*). Thomas Whalen's *Service* in the Scottish Pavilion North. The Exhibition produced many commissions for contemporary artists.

182. Archibald Dawson's *St Andrew* in the Scottish Pavilion South.

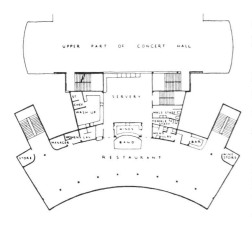

183 and 184 (*opposite*). Above, the monumental entrance to the United Kingdom Pavilion. Below, the enormous advertisement hoardings located on the Scottish Avenue.

185 and 186 (*above*). View down the Scottish Avenue to the Concert Hall (the hoardings are on the right); and the plan of the restaurant which fronted the Hall in a characteristic curve.

Great Scots like Robert Burns, Sir Walter Scott and Dr David Livingstone.

The theme of vigorous youth exemplified in so much of the Exhibition's statuary (for example, the idealised young giants outside the Canadian Pavilion) was very pronounced in the Social Services section in the South Pavilion, with its sculpture by Andrew Dods allegorising youth, and a giant composition of photographs of the many youth organisations which operated in Scotland. Fascination with youth and beauty - and the parallel obsession in the 1930s with health, daylight and fresh air - are hardly surprising in a society still marked by the carnage of the First World War and struggling, in Glasgow especially, to free itself from Victorian grime and industrial depression. Only in retrospect does the ardent desire for a new, healthier race become sinister, perverted by the Nazi pursuit of an Aryan Master Race.

The Second World War has also affected our opinion of architectural style. The Palace of Art which closed the east end of the Scottish Avenue, presiding over a small square, had the stripped classical appearance now associated with the monumental creations of Hitler's architect, Albert Speer. This was the only permanent building created for the Empire Exhibition, intended to continue as an art and exhibition gallery, so its construction was markedly different. Designed by Launcelot Ross to sketches by Tait, it suffers from the architect's attempt to produce something in keeping with the predominant style of the Exhibition, but in much heavier material, predominantly stone. The building comprised seven galleries around a central courtyard where sculpture was displayed. In keeping with its location on the Scottish Avenue and the third object of the Exhibition, the Palace of Art highlighted Scotland's rich artistic tradition. In the galleries Scottish painting from 1800 to the present was the predominant theme, although in the modern period the display opened up to encompass the work of many of the leading British painters of the day including Augustus John, William Russell Flint and Dame Laura Knight. Contemporary sculptors whose work was shown included Jacob Epstein, Thomas Whalen and Gilbert Bayes.

After the Palace of Art the visitor could spend a separate gate fee to escape modernity in the picturesque Clachan. This Highland Village was a descendant of the one so popular at Glasgow's Scottish Exhibition of 1911, but claimed to be larger. In some ways its historical accuracy was irrefutable, with exact reproductions of genuine cottages and a population of real Gaels, mending nets, making creels and spinning yarn. It was also

187 and 188. Two postcards from a set showing views of the Clachan. Above, the Chief's Castle which contained a hall for Highland entertainments, the loch before it winding into a painted backdrop. Below, a piquant contrast between the new and the old.

highly artificial, with burns meandering into painted stage-set landscapes, and like no Highland village anywhere contained buildings from Lewis, Skye and Argyll. The architect of the Clachan, Dr Colin Sinclair, had also included a house which was his proposal for the Highland dwelling of the future. By 1938 the idea of the standard house was well established, the first such having been produced by the Association for the Protection of Rural Scotland. This building, unlike all the others in the Clachan, actually conformed to contemporary building standards.

The contrast between the Clachan and the next structure on the tour, approached up a grand staircase complete with waterfall, could not have been more marked. On the summit of Bellahouston Hill rose a feat of engineering unlike any previously seen in Scotland - the Tower of Empire.

Although the tower was really no more than a lift shaft with viewing platforms it became a symbol for the whole Exhibition. By the time the Exhibition was open the Glasgow public had already given it the affectionate nickname of 'Tait's Tower'. And it was the tower which enchanted

189. Tait's Tower rises here above the exclusive Garden Club.

every visitor to the Exhibition. Descriptions of it abound with superlatives. Three hundred feet high, its silvered steel glittered by day and it shone out like a beacon at night. As an engineering achievement it was extraordinary. Because of the determination not to damage or remove trees, the space available for foundations was extremely limited: the Tower was literally anchored in an immense block of concrete weighing over three thousand tons, which is still inside Bellahouston Hill. The vane on top of the Tower served to counteract wind torque. This necessity was made a design feature and the resulting motif was repeated elsewhere in the Exhibition, notably in the towers of the Scottish Pavilions, and for sculptural effect beside the lake and cascades. At the base of the Tower curved the Treetops restaurant. Here Tait (following Joseph Paxton's example at the Crystal Palace in 1851) enclosed the mature trees on site within the buildings. Raising the restaurant on stilts allowed a clear route to the tower and gave diners the unique and enjoyable experience of eating among the treetops. At lunchtime on 13 October (a Thursday!) peace was disturbed when a 70 mph gust of wind blew in two of the restaurant's 20 ft high plate glass windows. Fortunately injuries were slight, though the flight of one diner, in a panic, necessitated a full scale search of the Exhibition which was called off a few hours later upon her return.

The Exhibition featured more than two hundred palaces and pavilions, many of them architecturally distinguished. Most critics however reserved their warmest praise for the exclusive Garden Club which stretched along the southern slope of the hill, occupying like its prede-

190. Taking tea in the Treetops restaurant: from a postcard.

191 and 192 (*opposite*). Above, the Tower casts its shadow over the trees as far as the North Bandstand. Below, the Tower and the Clachan again, in a juxtaposition which caught the popular imagination.

cessor in 1911 the most prominent site in the Exhibition. The inspiration for the design of this building undoubtedly came from Mendelsohn and Chermayeff's De La Warr Pavilion, Bexhill, Sussex (1935). Tait had been a judge of the competition which selected this submission, and his knowledge thus went well beyond the external appearance of the building and into the internal workings of the design. The Bexhill Pavilion was the first completely welded steel-framed structure in Britain. The use of an exterior cladding of prepared concrete sheets hung upon the frame suggests that this building was not only an influence on the design of the Garden Club, but may have been the structural precedent for the whole Empire Exhibition.

The Garden Club consisted of a rotunda containing six small shops where the public could purchase sweets and souvenirs, a linking colonnade (allowing access to the hill and tower behind), and a long low restaurant and club pavilion. 'The accommodation includes a glass cocktail bar, in which are featured tiny models of queer garden creatures, a lounge and restaurant', noted the *Official Guide*. The building featured some fine applied decoration with external sculpture by Hugh Lorimer and Thomas Whalen. Its main staircase inside circled round a pool which was intended to give a grotto effect with water spraying from the roof and a statuette by Norman Forrest as a centrepiece. The Club was open to all but the membership fee guaranteed exclusivity. Membership for the duration of the Exhibition was three guineas, reduced to two for those living more than 25 miles from Glasgow, with temporary membership for one week at one guinea.

Descending from the Garden Club back to his starting point at the Palace of Engineering, the visitor would certainly feel it was time to seek relief from education and awe in the simple excitements of what was billed as 'the biggest and most original amusement park in Europe'. This was certainly the most popular feature of the Exhibition and left behind some of the most cherished memories. With its large restaurant, Dance Hall and separate entrance it was self-contained, and segregated, as was customary, from the serious business of the Exhibition. Here Mr Butlin provided a wonderful variety of thrill rides and side-shows. These included a mile-long mountain switchback; the Crazy House with its optimistic 'For Sale' sign; the Great Carmo, 'Royal Magician'; an Indian Theatre, as there had been in 1901; and recalling 1911's popular West African Village, 'Savage West Africa', displaying Chief Mekewwhe and his Yoruba tribe. When Queen Mary paid an unscheduled visit to the Amusement Park in September consternation was caused by a mass exodus from rides still in motion to view the royal progress. The operators had the wit to switch off the electricity and no injuries resulted.

The Amusement Park was the end of a tour which though exhausting was by no means exhaustive. It certainly had not taken in the numerous individual pavilions of major companies. Some of the most prestigious were arranged in the fan-shaped area below the Garden Club, flanking the southern approach to the hill, others were out of the way, stuck in gaps on

193, 194 and 195. Three attractions in Butlin's Amusements Park: top, the mountain switchback, which ran like 1911's through scenery of painted canvas hung on scaffolding; middle, the Crazy House; bottom, the Indian Theatre (with the end of 'Savage West Africa' visible at the left).

196 (*opposite*). The clamour and fun of the Amusements Park evoked in this *Illustrated London News* sketch was a tremendous boost to spirits subdued by years of depression. The mile-long miniature railway shown in the foreground was actually operated with a 48 hp diesel-engined locomotive.

THE PEACE OF THE HIGHLAND CLACHAN —

THE HURLY-BURLY
OF THE AMUSEMENT PARK.

L

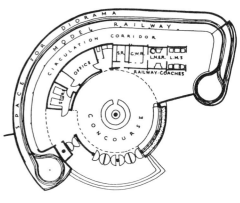

197 and 198. The drum-shaped Railways Pavilion and its ground plan.

the master-plan. Even in these small buildings Tait's system prevailed, and consistency of scale, materials and colours ensured that the homogeneity of the Exhibition was not disrupted. Many of the pavilions aspired to equal the excellence of architecture and design seen elsewhere in the Exhibition. ICI, the Empire's largest chemical producer, had a prominent location by the southern cascade for its fine pavilion by Basil Spence. Its three pylons represented air, earth and water, the fundamental raw materials of chemistry. Apart from its steel pillars and woodwork it was built entirely of ICI products. A little higher up the slope the Distillers Company had commissioned Tait himself to design what was appropriately enough one of the largest of the private pavilions, a magnet for supporters of the Scottish whisky industry.

It was not only industrial firms who erected pavilions: the TUC and the Ministry of Labour, for instance, were both exhibiting, though well separated. The churches were present too, the Church of Scotland and the Episcopalian Church with fairly conservative buildings, the Roman Catholic Church in a distinguished Pavilion by Jack Coia, and the Christian Scientists in a notable circular structure. Competing for hearts and minds on a different level were several newspapers: the *Glasgow Herald*, *Scotsman*, *Times*, *Daily Record*, *Daily Mail* and *Scottish Daily Express* all had their own buildings. The last shrewdly provided a crèche and children's playground, which may have increased its circulation among grateful parents.

In the British Railways Pavilion visitors could reserve tickets for anywhere in the Kingdom, and rail enthusiasts could watch scale models of famous trains travelling through the English, Scottish and Welsh country-

199. The Christian Science building.

200. The Atlantic restaurant, built round the granite memorial, still to be seen on Bellahouston Hill, which was unveiled by the King in 1937 to launch the Exhibition.

201. A detail from the ICI pool.

side. Another popular exhibit was the simulation in the City of Glasgow Pavilion (set back near the United Kingdom Pavilion) of a Corporation bus 'travelling' along a road which unrolled in front of the driver. The most distinguished visitor to come a cropper on this exhibit was Queen Mary, who drove into a tree.

The task of Queen Mary (who visited on more than one occasion, and to judge from numerous anecdotes evidently enjoyed the Exhibition) was to bestow royal patronage on some significant smaller pavilions. Of prestigious Glasgow companies the pavilion of James Templeton and Co., and the

202. Templeton's Pavilion: a strong contrast to their 1901 building (see 63).

203. One of the 50 electrically powered Lister auto-trucks which offered transportation round the site - here passing the *Scottish Daily Express* playground.

joint exhibit of Messrs Beardmore and Colville were singled out in mid September. In the first Queen Mary expressed admiration for a carpet costing £7 10s 0d, considered suitable for working-class homes and guaranteed to last twelve years. Among the more up-market carpets that were Templeton's traditional strength were samples of those made for her own Coronation in 1911 and for that of King George and Queen Elizabeth in 1937. Beardmore and Colville's shared enterprise, the Steel Industry, Scotland, Pavilion, was the largest of the private buildings. It featured a stainless steel fountain, a one ton block of coal, a steel plate almost 14 ft in diameter, and a 'cinema' where 'film with sound synchronisation' illustrated the work of the two great companies.[9]

In a city finally beginning to come to terms with the extent of its appalling housing problem, Queen Mary was also properly interested in the model working-class flats exhibited near the Clachan by the Council for Art and Industry. She admired their balconies, colour schemes and window seats, and enquired about their cost and the type of family for which they were intended. Others too were impressed by these three and four room dwellings with their 'well designed furniture and fittings from existing sources of supply'. There was talk of a Scottish local authority building them, and the plans were requested by London County Council. Next door Queen Mary visited the Cottage or Country House, the

204. An unusual close-up of the Tower, showing its corrugated skin.

Council's display of middle-class domestic architecture and furnishing. Designed by Basil Spence as an expression of practical utility, the house demonstrated the best that Scotland had to offer and care was taken to show a wide range of furnishing, fabrics and floor coverings, all of which could be ordered from the manufacturer.

As October drew to its end an almost royal welcome awaited its twelve millionth visitor. One little girl is alleged to have passed the turnstiles two hundred times hoping for the honour. But it was a Mrs Wilson who was presented with £10, a gold watch, and ironically, since she arrived two days before the Exhibition's close, a season ticket. On Saturday 29 October '"God Save the King" rang out from every part of the park, the Exhibition flag was lowered slowly on the floodlit tower, and the loudspeakers told the crowd that the Empire Exhibition (Scotland), 1938, was at an end.' This emotional occasion was accompanied by a cloud burst.

The Exhibition's organisers, who had once confidently expected up to 20 million visitors, had known for some time that the 15 million break-even attendance was out of reach. The final total was 12,593,232. Anxiety about impending war at the time of the Munich crisis was a significant factor, but the underlying problem was the weather. It was abominable that summer, cold, windy and wet. The guarantors lost 3s 5d in the pound, to their surprise and indignation. A plan to re-open the Exhibition in the summer of 1939, endorsed by Tait, who was confident that 'practi-

205. Night-time produced some breathtaking effects. Shown here is the North Cascade: its aerated waters were lit from beneath in changing colours. The Tower above shone with red, amber and green.

cally all the buildings of the Exhibition could easily be made to stand for another year', was mooted in early October 1938. Similarly a detailed proposal was prepared by the engineers of the Tower to secure the structure as a permanent monument for the City of Glasgow. However with war looming in Europe these and many other suggestions for the retention of some of the main buildings met with no success. The order to demolish the Tower was given in July 1939. A few buildings lingered on and were used as wartime transit shelters; some found their way into private hands for re-erection elsewhere.

The final announcement of war in the autumn of 1939 confirmed Glasgow's temporary economic recovery. But it damned the hope of peace expressed in the 'Objects of the Exhibition', and curtailed the fulfilment of the peaceful economic potential created by this enormous event. The virtual cessation of building work meant that the Exhibition's influence on the nation's architecture was dissipated. Indeed the Festival of Britain in 1951 was to take much of the credit for the introduction of new architecture to Britain. In other circumstances it might have been justly accorded to Tait's remarkable feat of efficient, appropriate and brilliant design. The events of history were against this, the grandest of Glasgow's Great Exhibitions. But financial loss and the dark days which followed should not dim the magnitude of its achievement. They have not dimmed the memories of those who marvelled that summer at the Empire Exhibition - at its fun and spectacle, its cascades, fountains and coloured lights, and above all at Tait's Tower, shining out in the night.

206. A sad farewell from the Exhibition's lion: logo from the invitation to the closing ball.

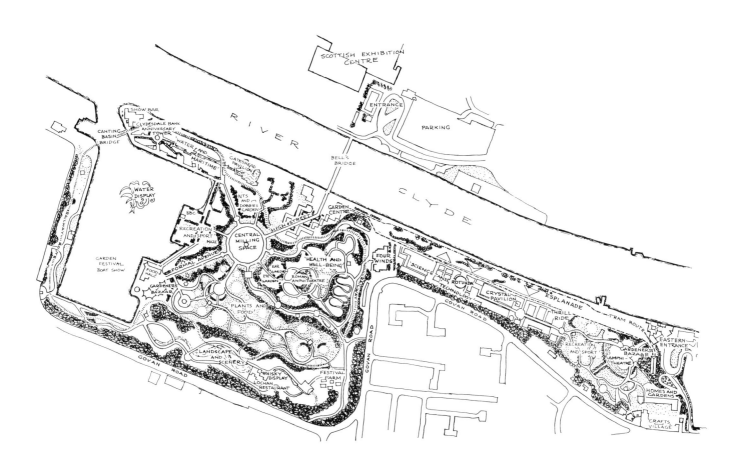

SCOTTISH EXHIBITION
CENTRE

ENTRANCE

PARKING

RIVER

CLYDE

BELL'S
BRIDGE

SHOW BAR

CLYDESDALE BANK
ANNIVERSARY
TOWER

CANTING
BASIN
BRIDGE

WATER AND
MARITIME

GATESHEAD
PAVILION

WATER
DISPLAY

GARDEN
CENTRE

PLANTS
AND
DOBBIES
GARDEN

HIGH STREET

BBC

RECREATION
AND SPORT
MAZE

CENTRAL
MILLING
SPACE

HEALTH AND
WELL-BEING

FOUR
WINDS

GARDEN
FESTIVAL
BOAT SHOW

FOOD
HALL

FORMAL AVENUE

EAR
GARDEN

ROMAN
AMPHITHEATRE

SCIENCE
AND
TECHNOLOGY

ROTUNDA

CRYSTAL
PAVILION

ESPLANADE

GARDENER'S
BAZAAR

PLANTS AND
FOOD

GOVAN ROAD

THRILL
RIDE

TRAM ROUTE

LANDSCAPE
AND SCENERY

GOVAN ROAD

RECREATION
AND SPORT

EASTERN
ENTRANCE

GARDENER'S
BAZAAR

WHISKY
DISPLAY

LOCHAN
RESTAURANT

FESTIVAL
FARM

GOVAN ROAD

AMPHI
THEATRE

HOMES AND
GARDENS

CRAFTS
VILLAGE

207. The Glasgow Garden Festival, 1988, held at Prince's Dock. (Based on the advance Masterplan.)

1988

208. The dramatically terrifying Thrill Ride, photographed in December 1987.

The Glasgow Garden Festival has been planned on the grand scale, billed as 'the UK's biggest single consumer event of 1988, an international occasion, which will rank alongside the great Empire Exhibition held fifty years ago'. Thus advance publicity set it in Glasgow's Exhibition tradition, and underlined the element which distinguishes this as something modern - its candidly commercial ethos. The 1938 Exhibition with its grand statements was the last fling of pre-war Europe. The only thing to attempt comparison later in the UK was the Festival of Britain in 1951, though giant Expos have been staged with varying degrees of success elsewhere in the world. While 1988's Garden Festival belongs to a genre only recently introduced to Britain, and still developing an appropriate

local form, there are many telling similarities with Glasgow's earlier Exhibitions. 1988 is in a sense their epilogue.

1938's Empire Exhibition appears most boldly in the publicity. Many people of course have living memories of Glasgow's last great show; but for other reasons too it seems more relevant. The Garden Festival shares its attempt to signify resurgence from a period of economic depression; its assertion that things can and will be better; its emphasis on a new start, and a new, more wholesome way of life. One hundred years on the industrial prosperity celebrated in 1888 seems remote, and perhaps still too painful to contemplate, as the vestigial remains of many of Scotland's great Victorian industries continue to disintegrate.

In the fifty years since the Empire Exhibition Glasgow has undergone a process of drastic change. Symbolically in the first post-war census in 1951 Glasgow lost to Birmingham the right to be called Second City, a title maintained for the previous 140 years. In conjunction with the Festival of Britain of the same year an Exhibition of Industrial Power was staged in the Kelvin Hall, on the site of the Machinery Hall of 1901. Attendance at 282,000 was only half the minimum hoped for. Despite a brief rebuilding boom, pride was at a low ebb, and the achievements of industry had lost their old magic. Successive attempts to plan a way out of the social and economic decline which followed have scarred the city's face

209. An early artist's impression of the proposed site. This appeared on the 1987 Glasgow telephone directory.

210 (*opposite*). The site taking shape, photographed in December 1987. The bridge is in place and the railway track can be clearly seen. The pyramidal building below the High Street is the Gateshead Pavilion, advertising Britain's next Garden Festival. Across the railway track the lavish National Trust for Scotland Garden and its pavilion are well advanced. At the top of the picture can be seen the great Finnieston crane, once used for loading locomotives onto ships.

1988

with tower blocks, swathes of motorways, and the derelict churches and cinemas of vanished communities. The old props of the economy have been virtually abandoned. Now at last as high technology, albeit supported by massive foreign investment, has replaced the old skills as a source of some prosperity, if not as an employer of manpower, there is hope that the corner has been turned. There is without doubt in many quarters a mood of optimism in the city (though it is seen by some observers as a 'false exuberance'). This the Garden Festival aims to enhance, along with the urban renewal which is the visible analogue of the new clean industries.[1]

Garden Exhibitions began in Germany, associated with the regeneration of devastated urban areas after the Second World War, and have continued there ever since, spreading to other European countries like the Netherlands, Belgium and France. The concept had been canvassed in the UK for some years by the horticultural industry and others and was being seriously pushed by Liverpool in 1981 when the Toxteth riots in July gave their case an irresistible cogency. Michael Heseltine at the Department of the Environment rapidly authorised the considerable public expenditure necessary to mount Britain's first two Garden Festivals, at Liverpool in 1984 and Stoke-on-Trent in 1986. In 1983 Glasgow began assembling a bid in competition with other places for a third event. While consultants, mindful in part of the centenary and jubilee which lay to hand, originally proposed 1988, by the time of the submission of *The Case for Glasgow* the target date had for various reasons been changed to 1989. It was only when the success of the Liverpool Festival was clearly established well on in 1984 that government decided to commit funds for a further series of events - at which point the Scottish Development Agency was asked whether it could manage 1988 (to be followed by Gateshead in 1990, and Somewhere in Wales, later identified as Ebbw Vale, in 1992). So the significant date is after all somewhat fortuitous.

The underlying objective of the Garden Festival is to boost the local and regional economy: it was not difficult to prove Glasgow's need in terms of blighted environment, unemployment and the loss of skilled workers. For this purpose the application of central government finance is now essential. The money has been channelled through the effectively independent Scottish Development Agency, of which The Glasgow Garden Festival 1988 Ltd is a wholly owned subsidiary. While the basic costs are being born by the SDA, the District and Regional Councils and the Chamber of Commerce are also heavily involved. Levels of sponsorship are high, expected to reach around £15 million, considerably more than Liverpool and Stoke together. In contrast to Glasgow's previous Exhibitions, this one is mounted in the confident expectation of a loss: of the £35 million expended it is anticipated that approximately £20 million will be recouped in revenues. But calculations are no longer straightforward. In return for the £15 million net cost of the Festival it is estimated that around £100 million will be injected into the economy. Where the previous essentially industrial Exhibitions assisted local manufacturing busi-

211. The site under construction, showing the star-shaped 'milling space' at the centre of the Festival's plan with the quaint reconstruction of a fisherman's cottage in the Argyll and Bute Garden nearby. The Clyde and the Canting Basin in the foreground are important assets for the site, as was the River Kelvin for earlier Exhibitions.

172

212. The Festival's logo.

nesses by offering a show-case, the direct commercial spin-off in 1988 will come almost exclusively from the servicing of the four million visitors expected. Around 300 jobs have been directly created in the preparatory period, and many more during the Festival itself.

Associated urban regeneration offers a more lasting return. World's fairs in general have frequently been planned to improve disused land and leave behind some public benefit (San Francisco in 1915, for example, rebuilding after its earthquake). The 'rules' of British garden festivals demand that the site should be 100 acres or more and derelict, and in an area in receipt of aid. Glasgow's housing problems and 'amenity deprivation' were manifest. The site chosen could not be more appropriate: almost 120 acres of Clydeside dockland, the epitome of the city's industrial heyday and its decline. When Prince's Dock was opened in 1900 it was the largest on the Clyde, designed to cope with sea traffic, and a potent symbol of the new century's misplaced optimism. Desolation followed but now it is literally flowering into new life. After the Festival the reclaimed land will be turned over rapidly to housing development and a permanent recreational facility. Negative land value has been suddenly converted to positive, with far-reaching effects. In addition the developers, Laing, who had cannily acquired the site in advance of the announcement of the

Festival, and are letting it back, have been offered a comparable acreage of sites elsewhere in the district to keep them occupied for its duration. This is represented as double the value in development terms, though the extremely advantageous conditions secured by Laing's have attracted adverse comment. The stock of private sector housing in Glasgow will be substantially increased. Beyond this the Garden Festival, like previous Exhibitions but more significantly, is prompting and accelerating numerous other projects. Stone-cleaning, painting, repairs and planting which might have been done eventually have been done in time for 1988. Renovation of Glasgow's architectural heritage is represented on site by the rehabilitation of the Four Winds building (which once housed hydraulic plant), and the two Clyde Harbour Tunnel rotundas on each side of the river, which have become restaurants.

Less tangible but as important today as it was in 1938 is the economic usefulness of the psychological boost offered by these major shows, with their lavish expenditure for effect. The displacement of 'Exhibition', with its perhaps too didactic and limited overtones, by the expansive, celebratory 'Festival' is part of the adaptation of such an event to modern circumstances. It is good for everyone to see a visible check in the downward spiral of cuts, shabbiness and loss of quality. The District Council for its part has allocated half a million pounds 'to create a citywide festival atmosphere', investing in projects and events that will make Glasgow 'look and feel good'. There is a determination to maximise the catalysing effect of the Garden Festival on the city as a whole and to enhance Glasgow's reputation as 'a place where good things are happening'.

Aggressive marketing over the last decade has greatly increased Glasgow's standing as a tourist centre. It now boasts eight out of the Scottish Tourist Board's top twenty attractions, including number one, the Burrell Collection. Again and again strangers drawn to Glasgow express surprise at what the city has to offer. As in 1888 tourism is seen as the key to changing Glasgow's poor image at home and abroad, and the Garden Festival has proved a powerful draw in 1988. Although there is a concern that the Festival be seen as properly national - the UK's festival, hosted by Glasgow - the exceptionally strong identity of the city has naturally imprinted itself and civic pride is once more at stake. In tones reminiscent of a century ago Glasgow's Garden Festival has been pitched against Liverpool's and Stoke's, and is confidently stated to be inaugurating a 'new generation' of garden festivals. Few doubt that attendance in 1988 will surpass Liverpool's 3.25 and Stoke's 2.18 million visitors. The Garden Festival has become an important part of the run-up to 1990, when Glasgow will be European City of Culture. (This is a City affair, though again the SDA was involved in presenting the well co-ordinated bid for nomination.)

Under the convention governing the frequency of major exhibitions Glasgow's Festival could not claim full international status: ten years must elapse after the Liverpool International Garden Festival in 1984 before Britain can mount another. (The Grand International Show of horticul-

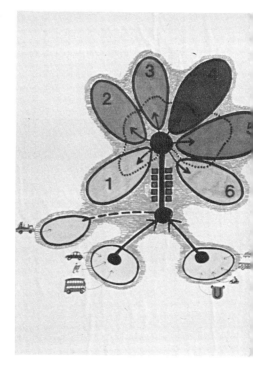

213. The design concept of the site is embodied in the Petal Diagram. The centre of the flower is the 'milling space', and the numbered petals represent the Theme Areas. The stem is the crucial retail area.

ture from 1-10 July does have international status as an indoor show.) But foreign participation has been zealously sought for the prestige it brings. The importance now attached to international relations is reflected in the wide range of countries involved, about 26 in all. National gardens and a number of 'Friendship Gardens' contributed by individual cities, will represent among others Germany, Israel, the USA, the USSR, the People's Republic of China and Japan. With the Olympic Games suffering from increasing political pressures such events as this offer a valuable arena for the old exhibition ideal of international harmony.

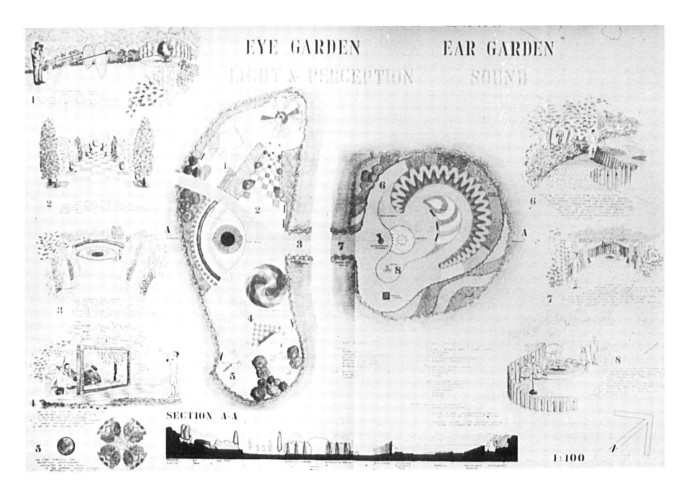

214. More design: the plan for the Glasgow District Council's Eye and Ear Gardens in the Health and Well-Being sector.

To the consumer the Festival offers 'a day out of this world', the slogan neatly expressing the important promise of release from everyday life. In 1988 advertising replaces the altruistically stated aims of Glasgow's earlier Exhibitions, and it homes in on for the first time on the 'fun factor'. 'Colour', 'sparkle', 'entertainment', 'excitement' and, constantly, 'unique' – these are the words which promote the Festival. The Exhibitions always offered these things, but in 1988 they are up front. Education remains significant but is subservient now to entertainment, not progress. On this level the Garden Festival is a carefully planned and expensively marketed leisure package.

While garden festivals are still an unfamiliar institution in Britain it has been important to get across to the public the scope of the enterprise, which is less limited to horticulture and closer to the concept of exhibitions than might be imagined, embracing displays of 'leading edge technology, sport, leisure and crafts'. The days are past when magnificent buildings can be run up for six months' use in the manner seen at the earlier Exhibitions. Landscaping and planting fulfil comparatively cheaply many functions of the big Exhibition buildings, laying out the structure of the Festival, loosely enclosing its different sections, and also providing the important 'special environment' - the element of colour and pleasure for the eye. Grandeur is no longer part of the brief. It is stressed that all plant material above bedding level will be reusable.

The garden theme might at first seem peculiarly alien to Glasgow - the city has fine parks, which reflect its municipal identity; but its history of dense industrialisation and tenement-dominated housing has excluded any tradition of private gardening. However it exemplifies the feeling that Glasgow has undergone a great change and has a new clean face to present to the world. 1938 also offered a bright new image; but a comparison of the two events reflects clearly the abandonment of planning on a grand scale for the less drastic solutions, more sensitive to conservation, which are so well expressed by the garden theme. 'Design', the obsession of the 1980s, pervades the Garden Festival.

The flower motif in the Festival's logo turns out to embody in an engaging manner its design concept. This is elucidated in the Petal Diagram. The Festival's 'roots' are the maintenance area, and the car parks

215 (*below*) and 216 (*opposite*). Artist's impressions were important for projecting major features to potential sponsors - the Clyde bridge, sponsored at a late stage by Bell's Whisky, and the Tower, early taken up by the Clydesdale Bank.

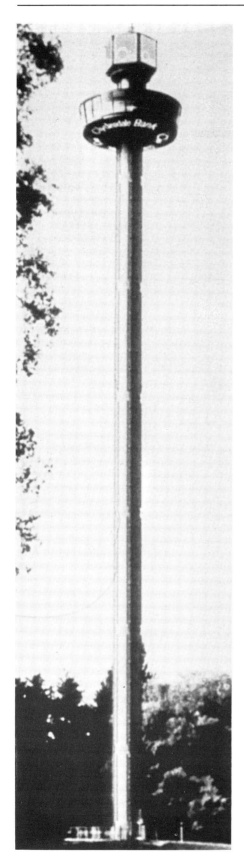

and other transport terminals whence visitors are sucked up the main retail section 'stem' to the 'eye of the daisy' - the great milling area. The 'petals' are the six Theme Areas. The site was planned in connection with an important permanent asset for Glasgow, the shiny new Scottish Exhibition and Conference Centre, opened in 1985, which houses some of the Festival's indoor shows and parallel events. Many visitors will enter from this direction, crossing the river on a new 120 m long footbridge with 'weather protection'. People like bridges, and this is an attraction in itself, illuminated at night by a double string of globes. Its cost exceeds a million pounds, of which about a quarter has been put up by Bell's Whisky. It can pivot open to allow the passage of ships, but will have to move after the Festival. The stream of visitors delivered this way at the top of the High Street 'funnel' fuses with those coming from the Festival's other entrance at the east end of the 'pan-handle', where they may have hopped onto a tram. The aim has been to plan a compact, well controlled site, which obeys the dictates of commercial design by delivering consumers as soon as possible to the retail area, and passing them out through it on exit.

In the sophisticated planning which has developed the Glasgow 'product' are incorporated many lessons learnt from careful analysis of its predecessors. Particularly instructive was the failure of Stoke. While poor marketing takes a share of the blame, it is clear that the site was too big, too open and insufficiently exciting. Glasgow's area (about 120 acres including 17 of water) is significantly smaller than Liverpool's and Stoke's (approximately 135 and 165 acres respectively), but more densely filled and designed for all-weather use. There are indoor show facilities near the Rotunda, as well as in the SECC. Great stress is being laid on a non-stop events programme, with an average of 65 performances a day - everything from stilt-walkers to string quartets, pipe-bands to ballet - and an emphasis on demonstrations in retail and display areas. The intention is to keep the site busy. The high level of sponsorship has also enabled more 'fun' features, important for the claim that this is 'Britain's liveliest ever festival' with a broad spectrum of appeal.

Aiming specifically at the 15-24 age-group found to be under-represented at Liverpool and Stoke the organisers have invested in a spectacular and very costly Thrill Ride, manufactured in the Netherlands. This horrendous 'white-knuckle' descendant of the dear old switchback demonstrates the rising thrill threshhold of modern generations. Here we see the beginning of an escalating amusement section which parallels the development of the Exhibitions: presumably all future garden festivals will have to spend on trumping Glasgow.

For the more sedate there is another spectacular feature not seen at the rival shows: a viewing tower, 64 m (240 ft) high (including antenna). This is likely to become a key image for the Festival, joining Tait's Tower of 1938 in a venerable tradition going back to Eiffel's unsurpassed contribution to the Paris Exposition of 1889, which has become the image building of its city. Towers are appropriately symbolic of renascence, aspiration, confidence. Glasgow's latest is emblazoned with the name and emblem of the Clydesdale Bank, celebrating the 150th anniversary of its establishment in the city. Grand gestures do not come cheap these days and sponsorship to the tune of half a million pounds must be visible. 1000 passengers per hour can travel in a ring-shaped cabin, rotating as it rises, up the slender tubular structure. Again, tellingly, it has been manufactured abroad, in Switzerland.

The other chief 'fun features', which also serve an essential purpose, tap nostalgia for forms of transport commonplace at the earlier Exhibitions: everyone loves the steam trains, and Glaswegians in particular love the trams. Three trains run on a 2 km circuit round the main site area, passing

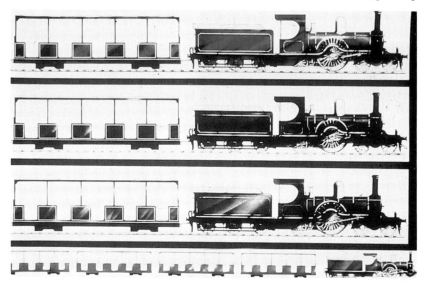

217 and 218. 'Steam' trains and trams have returned to Glasgow to carry visitors around the site.

219 (*opposite*). The first version (early 1987) of a publicity poster evoking a lavish, fun-packed site.

through a tunnel and crossing the Canting Basin on a novel floating bridge, calling at three stations. Modelled on the Caledonian Railway's 4-2-2 loco no. 123, which was built in Glasgow in 1886 and competed in 1888's railway races between Edinburgh and London, they are in fact diesels in disguise, complete with electronic effects. But the city which between 1852 and 1962 built 28,000 locomotives could not build these. The order was placed with Severn-Lamb Ltd of Stratford-on-Avon only weeks after British Rail closed its Springburn repair shop, bringing finally to an end one of Glasgow's greatest industries. Considerable difficulties have been overcome to revive five trams, which shuttle from the east end of the site to its High Street, serving five stops politically named for Scotland's New Towns. When Glasgow's last trams ran in 1962 people cried in the streets. The opening of the Transport Museum in its new home in Kelvin Hall, timed to coincide with the Festival, gives a further outlet for nostalgia. The Clyde has been revived as the recreational asset it was in the great days of the Clyde steamers, and boat trips should be popular. Various interesting vessels moored along Finnieston Quay opposite serve as 'wall-paper' to hide unsightly concrete at low tide.

In contrast to the earlier Exhibitions, retailing at the Festival is prominent and important, partly as a necessary pay-off for commercial sponsorship, but also in acknowledgement that spending money is one of today's

prime leisure activities, and that people like doing it in special surroundings. However there is concern to keep this under control and firmly
concentrated. The main shopping area is the Festival's High Street, designed by Glasgow architects Walter Underwood and Partners to incorpo-
rate famous local towers - Tron, University, Tolbooth Steeple, Trinity

220 and 221. Above, the west elevation of the High Street of small shop units, designed as a 'gentle caricature' of famous Glasgow buildings. Left to right: Tolbooth and the Glasgow School of Art entrance; Charing Cross Mansions; University Tower; and St Vincent St Free Church Tower and Templeton's Business Centre (the old carpet factory). The (genuine) Overton bandstand from Rutherglen, shown in the model opposite, provides a focal point and completes the Victorian image.

College, St Vincent St Church. This is reminiscent of 1911's popular Old Glasgow mock-up, though realism, which would be inappropriate as well as too expensive, has been replaced by bright effective scaffolding. With substantial rents and fitting out costs, and a 7-day week including evenings, retailers do not expect to make huge profits, but prestige and general promotion are thrown into the balance. There is another retail outlet for workers in the Craft Village near the east entrance, and souvenir shops and markets elsewhere on the site.

Supporting the fun and commerce are the six Theme Areas into which the site has been zoned: (1) Water and Maritime, (2) Landscape and Scenery, (3) Plants and Food, (4) Health and Well-Being, (5) Science and Technology, and (6) Recreation and Sport (split into two areas, water at the west and land at the east end of the site). Linking the sections are three winding Theme Trails - History and Heritage, Education and Culture, and Horticulture. Although their content is projected as 'educational', the Theme Areas were conceived to counter the difficulty found by many firms in identifying with a garden festival at Liverpool and Stoke. The divisions are elastic enough to appeal to any possible sponsor. At another level the categories compare interestingly with the classification of the earlier Exhibitions. The twin pillars of Industry and Art have vanished. In place of a world confidently exploited and enclosed for exhibition the displays now explore man's ambiguous relationship with his environment. Questions are posed where previously all was taken for granted. This is a trend which began after the Second World War, and was strikingly embodied in the Montreal Expo of 1967.

'Art', which has lost its unchallenged status and the rôle in public propaganda so noticeable in 1938, will be scattered informally around the site. The word 'Industry' has been almost totally suppressed, felt to conflict with the Festival's image. Science and Technology have taken up the theme of human inventiveness, an emphasis first seen at Chicago in 1933-4 and standard in post-war expos. But this displacement of the prestige of industry by hi-tech is particularly relevant to Glasgow's recent development and hopes for the future. Even then the displays of technology in the spectacular Crystal Pavilion will be interlarded with games and gadgets lest they deter visitors by seeming too educational. It is in the Health and Well-Being sector that the Bank of Scotland and Hewden Stuart have jointly sponsored a large building and garden on the theme of great Scottish inventors. The Clyde's shipbuilding history features in the Water and Maritime section, but exotica like a Viking longship and a Chinese junk will probably have more appeal. This is after all a garden festival: industrial involvement is normally in the form of contributions in kind (e.g. bricks for the stations) or more commonly large sums of money. Tate and Lyle, for instance, the owners of Scotland's last surviving sugar-refinery at Greenock, have sponsored one of the trains with £75,000.

A few survivors, or at least inheritors, of some of the local industries which were so prominent at earlier Exhibitions will be in evidence again. There were indeed specific attempts to approach firms which had shown in 1938, though few survive in recognisable form. Weir's is one notable name that persists, and its 150 ft illuminated water spout in the Canting Basin recalls the firm's showy waterfall in 1901. Stoddard Templeton, the Elderslie company which absorbed Glasgow's great carpet manufacturer, is providing carpets in the majority of Laing's 13 show houses, and is one of approximately 20 Scottish manufacturers to exhibit in the Bank of

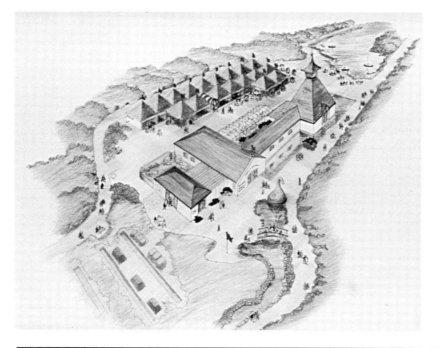

222. Artist's impression of the Distillery.

Scotland building. Whisky continues to be a major and vital Scottish export and the firm of Stanley P. Morrison has constructed an attractive representation of its Speyside Distillery in the Landscape and Scenery sector. (The Temperance campaigners so active at the first Exhibitions have lost the day and alcohol will be freely available.) Responsible attitudes are however paraded in the involvement of Scottish Agricultural Industries Ltd in the exhibit, showing the careful exploitation of whisky's waste products. It is the tobacco industry, perfectly blameless in 1938, which is now the object of public disapproval: Glasgow has recently embarked upon a campaign to become a 'smokeless' city. Aware of this the industry did not come forward for sponsorship, nor was it approached.

Among corporate bodies which appeared in 1938 are two which feel the need for self-promotion even more keenly today: British Rail and the Church. The first has involved itself fully for the first time with a garden festival, with a substantial 'Rail Pavilion' within the Festival, and an extensive environmental clean-up of its property outside it - bridges, trackside, stations - as well as lavish assistance with advertising. The different Churches separately represented in 1938 have joined with other denominations and organisations and seized the opportunity for a demonstration of modern ecumenical neighbourliness in the jointly funded Church Garden, intended to provide a haven for meditation in the busy site. This element of co-operation is common to nearly all the exhibits, generally uniting the public and private sectors to give the blend of altruism and commercial advantage which has always been characteristic of exhibitions. It is prompted chiefly by the extreme costliness of such displays today. Sponsors and projects have been skilfully married up and steered towards good taste by 'PDT', the Product Development Team. The prestigious National Trust for Scotland Garden, for instance, is being supported by about 25 sponsors, chief among them Dobbies.

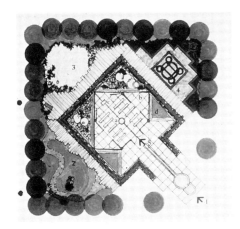

223. The ecumenical Church Garden.

The element of social conscience sets the Festival in the exhibition tradition and distinguishes it from a Theme Park. Two bungalows for the handicapped shown by the Scottish Special Housing Association can be compared with 1901's Sunlight Cottages and the model working-class flats of 1938. A model house today is a low energy house, as exhibited by the South of Scotland Electricity Board. Electricity at the earlier Exhibitions represented excitement and a promise of boundless energy. Now it is an essential part of everyday life and too precious to be wasted. This awareness of the environment and the value of the world's now limited resources is central to the Garden Festival and quite different from the attitudes which informed the previous occasions. The Forestry Commission, which in the eyes of many has had such a deleterious effect on Scotland's natural landscape, is shrewdly courting public approval with its major 'Magic Forest' display. This attempts among other things to show the woodland from the point of view of its animal inhabitants, and is aimed specifically at children.

The awareness of children's needs is characteristic of this modern exhibition (and indeed distinguishes the British from the more grown-up

German tradition in garden festivals). A key selling point has been its offer of 'something for all the family'. This has always been a practical attraction of the Glasgow Exhibitions, even if the orientation was clearly towards the adult. Nowadays children's tastes take precedence. This is partly because they give powerful access to the parental pocket; but it is also understood that if the kids are happy the adults are generally happy too. Crêches and play areas have been provided and many exhibits are geared specially to children or carefully designed to include them: Stirling District Council for instance offers a mystery maze with 'surprise features

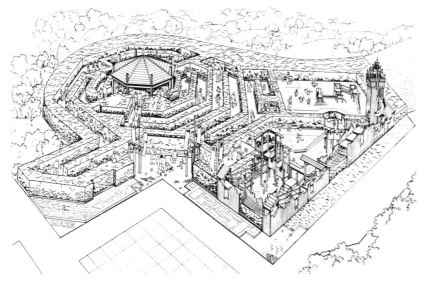

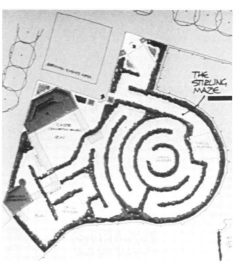

224 and 225. The Stirling Maze, offering plenty of entertainment for children, and its plan.

to delight all age groups' and 'stunning audio-visuals' to package its historical propaganda for Stirling. Strathclyde Regional Council is exploiting the educational potential of the Festival and school parties will account for a sizeable proportion of its visitors. Attractive presentation of instructive material has long been a feature of exhibitions, but techniques are now necessarily more sophisticated. Simple wonder is a reaction much harder to evoke than in the days before television in any but the very young.

The marketing of the event has always been a strong point of Glasgow's Exhibitions, even when it was the responsibility of amateurs. The Garden Festival's enormous promotion drive with a budget of well over £2 million has been undoubtedly effective. There has been a carefully managed operation to communicate the broad scope of the Festival and generate excitement about particular features, especially its programme of events. Packaging to the travel trade in a way not seen at the earlier garden festivals is expected to bring in around a million outsiders. Here Glasgow can capitalise again on the distinctive tourist appeal of Scotland and the wide dispersal of Scots blood, which makes the Festival much easier to sell outside the region than Liverpool's or Stoke's.

Marketing to the local population has perhaps been too effective. 78,000 season tickets, greatly in excess of the 50,000 target, were sold in a promotion drive to the end of July 1987. At £15, only three times the standard entry charge of £5, they were undoubtedly cheap: the price then rose

226. A computer's projection of the Crystal Pavilion by Bruce, Patience and Wernham. Loosely based on the hexagonal quartz crystal, the building is claimed as the largest silicon-method structure in the UK to date, and is constructed in three tints of blue glass.

by stages to £45. At the time of writing around 100,000 sales are in prospect. This compares with a total of about 32,000, including a few thousand sold cut-rate towards the close at Liverpool, and a mere 8,250 at Stoke, which indeed fell far below its attendance target. Each ticket is reckoned to produce 10-15 visits. The heavy early sales at Glasgow were valued for securing 'commitment' to the Festival, a goal undoubtedly achieved. But with so very many free to come and go as the fancy takes them the problem of unpredictable troughs and surges in attendance will be exacerbated, and the site's facilities will doubtless come under strain on good days, as they did for instance in 1901, when around 80,000 season tickets were sold.

Now it all really depends on the weather. The planners are prepared for whatever comes, with a system of private bore-holes and storage tanks to meet a drought such as parched Liverpool, and shelter every fifty paces and a big programme of indoor events for what is assumed as the more likely possibility, the bad weather which so damaged Stoke. The Empire Exhibition of 1938 suffered what was said to be the worst summer in the region for a hundred years. But the first three Exhibitions were so blessed by heaven that it was proposed that to secure a good summer Glasgow had only to mount one of its Great Exhibitions. It can only be hoped that the old tradition is revived in 1988, as the City's motto, 'Let Glasgow Flourish', is given a hopeful new meaning.

EPILOGUE

Exhibitions of the sort we have been describing reflect the ethos and aspirations of the society which creates them; and they have always been good for people. They present an ideal version of the real world - regulated, in working order, proposing limitless possibilities for mankind and full of good things for the consumer. It is always reassuring to know that society can mount something so spectacular, on a scale suggesting command of infinite resources. Their temporary nature is essential to the effect: that so much magnificence has only six months to live provokes intense emotions.

Glasgow's Great Exhibitions, like all others, have both expressed an identity and offered temporary release from the ordinariness of daily life. The richly ornamented grandeur of 1888 and 1901 afforded an escape from industrial grime to oriental exoticism, while it reflected the city's Victorian self-confidence and Glasgow-centred cosmopolitanism. The historical fancy-dress of 1911 turned to the make-believe past, and sank Glasgow's distinctive identity in general Scottish nationalism. 1938 by contrast projected a message from the government, promising escape to a brave new streamlined future, built on health and youth; Glasgow was advertised as a great British city at the heart of a speciously united Empire. In 1988 green and pleasant gardens offer the antithesis of urban dereliction, and as a new life springs up among the ruins of the industrial past, Glasgow, looking again to itself, projects an attractive image appropriate to a new era.

Over the last one hundred years Glasgow's Great Exhibitions have expressed the city's unquenchable optimism. They have galvanised its proud spirit of self-help, enhanced its reputation and left behind a legacy of solid improvements. But one should not be too solemn about this. Their most potent gift to millions has been the recollection of fun. If it is the price of sandwiches, the queues for lavatories, heat, rain and sore feet that people notice most at the time, what abides in the memory is the spectacle, the gaiety, the amusements and illuminations - the intoxicating sense of participation in a special and unrepeatable occasion.

NOTES

1888

1. This sounds familiar after government attempts to revive the concept, in theory at least, in the 1980s. In the interim these valuable links have been broken. The Art Gallery and Museum is run by Glasgow District Council while art and technical education is now under the control of Strathclyde Regional Council.
2. *Quiz* 25 May 1888, p. 116.
3. Roger Billcliffe, *The Glasgow Boys* (John Murray 1985) includes a chapter on the 1888 Exhibition, pp. 207-31.
4. *Builder* 54 (1888) 26 May, p. 370.
5. Both views found in *The Builder*: 54 (1888) 19 May, p. 353; 26 May, p. 369.
6. *Art Journal*, Glasgow Exhibition special number (July 1888) p. 13.
7. *Builder* 55 (1888) 4 Aug., p. 82 (both quotations in this paragraph).
8. *Quiz* 21 Sept. 1888, p. 21.
9. *Exhibition Weekly Journal* 1 (26 May 1888) p. 10.
10. *Art Journal* (n. 6) p. 5; a fuller version by the same hand in T. Raffles Davison, *Pen-and-Ink Notes* p. 121.
11. *Bailie* 27 June 1888, Exhibition supplement p. 4.

1901

1. In the interim Glasgow's first East End Exhibition had been held in 1890-1 (25 Dec. - 21 April), in the Old Reformatory Building off Duke Street. Attendance was 747,873, and roughly £3000 was raised towards the People's Palace, which was opened on Glasgow Green in 1898 to cater for the people of this less privileged part of the city.
2. J. K. McDowall in the preface to his *People's History of Glasgow* (Glasgow 1899).
3. *Official Guide*; *Builder* 62 (1892) p. 318.
4. *Exhibition Illustrated* 1 (4 May) p. 7.

5. Preface to D. S. McColl, *Nineteenth Century Art* (Glasgow 1902), illustrated with pictures from the Fine Art collection of the Exhibition.
6. *Studio* 23 (1901) p. 48.
7. Stands for the GSA, Pettigrew and Stephens, Francis Smith and Rae Bros, illustrated in Roger Billcliffe, *Charles Rennie Mackintosh* (Lutterworth Press 2nd edn 1980) pp. 103-4; or *Mackintosh Furniture* (Lutterworth Press 1984) pp. 76-7. Drawings signed by Mackintosh submitted by Honeyman and Keppie in the architecture section attracted some critical approval.
8. W. G. Riddell, *The Thankless Years* (London/Glasgow 1948): we are grateful to John Burnett for drawing this book to our attention.
9. John Shearer, *Exhibition Illustrated* 1 (4 May) p. 15.
10. James McFarlane, *Exhibition Illustrated* 6 (8 June) p. 133.
11. Paul Rothenburg, who was convener of the Foreign Committee in both 1888 and 1901, interviewed in *Exhibition Illustrated* 5 (1 June) p. 110. As a Royal Commissioner for Britain at Paris he was able to gather many exhibits for Glasgow.
12. *The Artist* Sept. 1901, pp. 26, 28; the accusations of this 'advanced' magazine were directed mainly at the contents of the Industrial Hall, where the pavilion of Whylie (*sic*) and Lochhead was the only thing thought worthy of attention.
13. *News* 9 March. Main coverage in the *Builder*, *Studio*, *Art Journal* and *Architectural Review*. See also Catherine Cooke's monograph 'Fedor Osipovich Shekhtel', *AA Files* 5 (Jan. 1984), esp. pp. 4-8.
14. *Exhibition Illustrated* 6 (8 June) p. 133.

1911

1. 1903-4 had seen the second East End Exhibition (9 Dec. - 9 April), which was

held to raise money for the Royal Infirmary, 'to display and encourage the work of the artisan classes', and to provide entertainment for the East End of the city. Attendance totalled 908,897, but the profit was only £221 18s 6d.

2. Resolution of a meeting held on 3 March 1909, quoted in the Exhibition prospectus.

3. *Builder* 100 (1911) 12 May, p. 575.

4. Walker had worked on the 1901 Exhibition under Miller (he designed the Canadian Pavilion), and his firm had since done exhibitions at Wolverhampton (1902) and Edinburgh (1908).

5. *Glasgow Herald* 2 May.

6. Teddy bears were named for Theodore Roosevelt around 1907.

7. G. Eyre Todd, *Leaves from the Life of a Scottish Man of Letters*, has chapters on the pageants, pp. 151-6, and the Exhibition, pp. 171-81.

8. *Builder* 100 (1911) 12 May, p. 575.

9. *Glasgow Herald* 9 May.

10. The tart description of a correspondent in the *Evening Citizen* of 31 May.

11. A letter from 'Disgusted', *Glasgow Herald* 15 May.

1938

1. Cecil M. Weir, Convener of the Council of Management.

2. Quoted in the *Glasgow Herald* 26 Feb. 1937, p. 7.

3. T. S. Tait, 'Planning the Empire Exhibition', *SMT & Scottish Country Life* (May 1938).

4. J. M. Richards, 'Glasgow 1938: a critical survey', *AR* Glasgow Exhibition special number (July 1938).

5. J. R. Allan, *The Scottish Field* (May 1938) p. 21.

6. The primrose suite ended its days in a house in University Gardens, but was removed and probably destroyed on its conversion to departmental use by Glasgow University. The building is now occupied by the Department of Art History, which may lament the loss of this very particular treasure.

7. *Glasgow Herald* 6 Sept., p. 10.; Richards, *AR* (n. 4).

8. *Glasgow Herald*, Empire Exhibition special number p. 23.

9. Other commercial pavilions are too numerous to detail, but among names still familiar today were Dunlop, Chiver's, Esso, Shell-Mex, and the Glasgow firm of Glenfield and Kennedy.

1988

1. We commend Ian Jack's essay, 'The repackaging of Glasgow', dated 1984, and now published in his volume of selected journalism *Before The Oil Ran Out: Britain 1977-86* (Secker & Warburg 1987) pp. 200-20.

SURVIVING BUILDINGS AND FEATURES

With a few exceptions Glasgow's Great Exhibitions have vanished without trace. The structures were essentially temporary, though people were loath to part with them: some were re-erected but have not survived the passage of time. Materials and fittings were sold off after the events and must persist in considerable quantity, often unrecognised. There are indeed many reports of surviving buildings and features but few can be properly substantiated.

1888

The Doulton Fountain. This was moved to Glasgow Green and still stands there, but in a state of terminal disrepair, a sorry reminder of the imperial grandeur of the Exhibition.

The Fairy Fountain. According to the archives the fountain (presumably without its electrical works) was purchased at the Exhibition and removed to Maryborough, New South Wales, Australia, where it can apparently still be seen.

The Machinery Hall. Allegedly re-erected at Dalmarnock: the materials at least may be re-used. Now derelict.

Exhibition Office, 50 Gray Street. Now a private house.

1901

The Kelvingrove Art Gallery and Museum. Begun with the proceeds of Glasgow's first International Exhibition, and opened at its second, this is a fine memorial to both events. It houses the best municipal art collection in the country.

The Saracen Fountain. This cast iron fountain was named for Walter Macfarlane and Co.'s Possilpark foundry, and presented to the City. It was later moved to Alexandra Park, where it still stands.

The Sunlight Cottages. The pair of model cottages on the pattern of those built by Lever for the employees at Port Sunlight can be seen *in situ* in Kelvingrove Park.

227. 'India', a detail from the Doulton Fountain. Its condition has further deteriorated since this record was made in 1981.

1911

An Clachan Memorial. This marks the site of the Exhibition's popular Highland Village in Kelvingrove Park.

Bandstand and Amphitheatre. The bandstand visible today is a 1920s replacement for the original one handed over to the Corporation.

1938

The Palace of Art. Designed as a permanent building, to serve as an exhibition gallery in Bellahouston Park, it survives for 'recreational' use.

The Palace of Engineering. Re-erected for use by Scottish Aviation at Prestwick Airport.

The South African Pavilion. This was rebuilt at ICI's Nobel plant at Ardeer, where it serves as a staff dining room.

The Exhibition Memorial. A block of granite in Bellahouston Hill, unveiled by King George VI in 1937, commemorates the building of the Exhibition.

The Peace Cairn. Remains *in situ* in Bellahouston Park.

228. The Palace of Art today in Bellahouston Park.

1988

At the time of writing negotiations are still in progress about the fate of the Festival's various structures in the face of Laing's plans for speedy redevelopment of the site for private housing. There is a natural wish to salvage some of the immense effort and expense invested in it. The Crystal Pavilion is 'demountable' and there are hopes that it will find a permanent site in Glasgow as a 'Crystal World' attraction. Other features will have some afterlife: the High Street's glasshouses, for instance, used to house shop-units, were designed to be saleable to the City Parks and Recreation Department.

Clyde Harbour Tunnel Rotundas and Four Winds Building. These are listed buildings which have been rehabilitated for the Garden Festival.

Bell's Bridge. The future of this expensive structure is uncertain. It will probably be relocated.

SOURCES AND SELECT BIBLIOGRAPHY

Our main sources have been the catalogues, guides, daily programmes and publicity material issued for the separate Exhibitions; contemporary newspapers and periodicals; committee minutes; and memoirs.

Pre-eminent among newspapers covering this period is *The Glasgow Herald* (published under this name from 1805), together with the *Glasgow Weekly Herald* (1854-1938). We have also found *The Bailie* (1872-1926), Glasgow's answer to *Punch*, particularly useful. Alongside is a bewildering number of local papers, which we attempt to list here for interest and convenience.

The North British Daily Mail (1851-1900), becoming *The Glasgow Daily Mail* (Jan. to June 1901), then included in the *Daily Record*; *The Evening Citizen* (1864-1914), becoming *The Glasgow Citizen* (to 1923), before reverting to *The Evening Citizen*, and *The Glasgow Weekly Citizen* (1877-1912); *The Evening Times* (1877 onwards); *The Glasgow Observer* (1885-1968); *The Glasgow Evening News* (1888-1905), becoming *The Glasgow News* (to 1915), then *The Evening News* (to 1957); *The Daily Record* (1895 onwards); *The Glasgow Examiner* (1895-1903), becoming *The Glasgow Star and Examiner* (to 1937); *The Scots Pictorial* (1897-1903), becoming *The Social Pictorial* (1903-6), reverting to *Scots Pictorial* (1906-23), then amalgamated with *The Bulletin*; *The Weekly Record* (1899-1902), becoming *The Glasgow Weekly Record* (in 1902), then *The Scottish Weekly Record* (1902-15); *The Bulletin* (1915-23), becoming *The Bulletin and Scots Pictorial* (Jan. 1924-1960).

Among national periodicals covering all the Exhibitions *The Illustrated London News*, *The Architectural Review* and *The Builder* are worthy of special mention.

Illustrations are an invaluable source of information. Here we are indebted to the fine photographs of T. & R. Annan, official photographers in 1888, 1901 and 1911: with a few fortunate exceptions the negatives are lost, though souvenir albums for 1901 and 1911 were published. J. M. Lawson was appointed for the Empire Exhibition in 1938. Picture postcards appeared between the first two Exhibitions and are very useful. Sketches in the *The Bailie*, covering the first three Exhibitions, are both entertaining and revealing about social aspects of the Exhibitions.

We indicate below the main additional sources for the individual Exhibitions. A few others are mentioned in the notes to each chapter.

1888

The Victorian passion for information meant that this Exhibition was fully described and reported. Coverage in *The Builder*, for example, is excellent. Catering for the general public *The Illustrated London News*, with its fine engraved illustrations, is particularly distinguished; its rivals *The Pictorial World* and *The Graphic* are also good. We publish for the first time many photographs, presumably by Annan, from a record of the Exhibition held in the Special Collections of the University of Glasgow Library.

Quiz (1881-98): a Glasgow weekly rival to *The Bailie*, with good art criticism, and some excellent sketches by 'Twym' (A. S. Boyd), which were also published as *Twym's Scraps*.

T. Raffles Davison, *Pen-and-Ink Notes at the Glasgow Exhibition* (Glasgow 1888): line drawings by this noted illustrator and general description by Robert Walker. The same pair was responsible for the *Art Journal* special number.

The Exhibition Weekly Journal: a gossipy sheet, claiming to be the first such journal, printed within the Exhibition. It apparently did not survive beyond its second number (2 June).

The Great Exhibition of '88. Frolic and Fun That's Done for Those That Would Wait (Glasgow 1888): a collection of cartoon sketches, many of which we have used.

1901

As an international exhibition this event attracted good coverage in the many 'art' magazines which flourished at this period, especially *The Art Journal*, *The Artist*, *The Studio*, and *The Magazine of Art*, as well as in specialist periodicals like *The Architectural Review* and *The Builder*.

The Exhibition Illustrated: a weekly magazine, well illustrated, with interviews, items on different exhibits and a pleasantly sardonic 'Notes and News' section. Unfortunately publication ceased, somewhat mysteriously, with the number for 3 August.

1911

This Scottish Exhibition was largely ignored by the national magazines mentioned above, but coverage in Scottish newspapers was good. Scrapbooks in the Kelvingrove Art Gallery and Museum Library have been a useful resource.

G. Eyre Todd, *Leaves from the Life of a Scottish Man of Letters* (Glasgow 1934): memoirs of one of the instigators and organisers of the Exhibition.

1938

The Empire Exhibition was widely reported and photographed. We have taken many of our illustrations from a fine set of unpublished colour slides by George Allan.

The Glasgow Herald (which also published an Empire Exhibition special number) and *The Bulletin* have been basic sources; also *The Scottish Field*, *SMT and Scottish Country Life*, and *The Weekly Illustrated*. Once again *The Illustrated London News*, *The Architectural Review* and *The Builder* are good. Various souvenir publications are also useful.

J. Neil Baxter, *Thomas S. Tait and the Glasgow Empire Exhibition 1938* (MA thesis, University of Glasgow 1982): explores the influence of the Architect-in-Chief upon the architecture of the Exhibition.

1988

Our information on the Garden Festival derives from interviews, material supplied by contributors, and advance publicity.

General reading on international exhibitions

Allwood, John, *The Great Exhibitions* (Studio Vista 1977). The only general book in English; a very well illustrated survey of world's fairs. (The treatment of Glasgow is limited and unfortunately includes a few errors.) Bibliography.

Altick, R., *The London Shows* (Harvard 1986). A fat and fascinating book. Bibliography.

Benedict, Burton, *The Anthropology of World's Fairs: San Francisco's Panama Pacific International Exposition of 1915*, with contributions by M. J. Dobkin *et al.* (Scolar Press 1983). A stimulating discussion of the phenomenon of world's fairs from the anthropological point of view, followed by essays on the SF Exposition.

Victoria and Albert Museum. *The Great Exhibition of 1851*, by C. H. Gibbs-Smith (HMSO 1950; 2nd edn 1981). Good introduction, illustrations with full captions. Bibliography.

The social and economic background

A brief selection of generally accessible books. All include useful suggestions for further reading.

Berry, Simon, and Whyte, Hamish, eds, *Glasgow Observed* (John Donald 1987)

Campbell, R. H., *Scotland since 1707: the rise of an industrial society* (Basil Blackwell 1971)

Checkland, Sydney and Olive, *Industry and Ethos: Scotland 1832-1914*, New History of Scotland 7 (Edward Arnold 1984)

Cunison, J. and Gilfillan, J. B. S., eds, *The Third Statistical Account of Scotland. Glasgow* (Collins 1958)

Daiches, David, *Glasgow* (André Deutsch 1977)

Gibb, Andrew, *Glasgow: the making of a city* (Croom Helm 1983)

Harvie, Christopher, *No Gods and Precious Few Heroes: Scotland 1914-1980*, New History of Scotland 8 (Edward Arnold 1981)

Hibbert, Christopher, *Illustrated London News Social History of Victorian Britain* (Angus and Robertson 1975)

McKean, Charles, *The Scottish Thirties: an architectural introduction* (Scottish Academic Press 1987)

Oakley, C. A., '*The Second City*' (Blackie 1946; 2nd edn 1967; 3rd edn 1975)

Smout, T.C., *A Century of the Scottish People 1830-1950* (Collins 1986)

INDEX

197

ILLUSTRATION ACKNOWLEDGEMENTS

For permission to reproduce illustrations we gratefully acknowledge the following: Sandy Allan (Nos 167-71, 176, 180, 183-5, 191-5, 203, 205); T. & R. Annan and Sons, Ltd, Glasgow (11, 60, 120, 145); *Architectural Review* (197) and Sir Hugh Casson (159, 186, 198, 201); Andrew Baxter (1, 54, 110, 152, 207); Neil Baxter (9, 55, 58, 61-3, 75, 83, 86-7, 89, 93, 96, 100-1, 104, 113, 127, 132-3, 139, 149, 151, 157, 158, 162, 175, 182, 187-9, 204, 206); Bovis Construction Ltd (208, 210-11); Bruce, Patience and Wernham (226); Edward Chisnall, Bell-in-the-Tree (219); Catherine Cooke (97); Crouch and Hogg (215); Michael Davidson (126); Dr Ian Evans (5, 56-7, 84, 112, 121-2, 135, 140-2, 144, 146, 150); Glasgow Art Gallery and Museum (frontispiece, 68-9); K. J. Fraser, Director of Parks and Recreation, Glasgow District Council (214); Glasgow Garden Festival Ltd (209, 216, 218); Gillespie's (212-13, 223); The Hunterian Art Gallery, University of Glasgow (59, 78, 136-7); The Illustrated London News Picture Library (51, 196); Barclay Lennie (front cover, 23, 66, 76, 79, 85, 103, 105, 108, 111, 115-16, 119, 125, 128, 138-9, 147-8); McKay and Forrester (222); The Mitchell Library, Glasgow (2, 10, 15, 16, 20, 39, 49, 52-3, 90, 106, 123, 143); The People's Palace Museum, Glasgow 130, 227); Severn-Lamb Ltd (217); Douglas Thornton, Stirling District Council (224-5); Sir John Summerson (179); William Topping (back cover, 153-4, 160-1, 163-6, 173-4, 181, 199-200); Walter Underwood and Partners, Glasgow (220-1); The University of Glasgow Library (17-19, 22, 24, 26, 30-1, 33, 36-7, 42, 44, 46). We thank all of the above for their kind assistance.